Don't wait 'til you graduate

The

Canadian

job search

guide

for the

real world

Stephen J. Kaplan

CACEE · ACSEE

PUBLISHED BY:

CACEE • ACSEE
Canadian Association of Career Educators and Employers
Association canadienne des spécialistes en emploi et des employeurs
1209 King Street West, Suite 205
Toronto, Ontario M6K 1G2

To my best friend Jody,
for being a great inspiration
and helping my dream
to come true.
To Jody and Julia,
for making this the
best summer of my life.

Acknowledgements

This book would never have been possible without support, understanding and encouragement from many people. My sincere thanks to:

The Executive Committee of CACEE who thought this was a great idea and believed I could do it.

Heather Schwartz whose excellence, dedication, tireless efforts, and persistence on the phone, were truly outstanding. On-campus recruiters beware, armed with all this knowledge, Heather is in the job market this fall.

Ted Haiplik and Liga Liepa who proved to me what the phrase "extraordinary friends" really means.

Melanie King for being a marvellous editor.

Doreen Knol, Bruce Walker, Colleen Bronson and Jody Goodman for their insightful feedback and speedy reading.

Joel Shalit, Bonnie Frank and Lori Vinebaum for helping us in a pinch.

Gina Roitman for her humour and insight, and for providing *Don't wait 'til you graduate* with a home during its conception.

Joan Fraser for being a creative genius and for interpreting my thoughts so well.

The University of Tennessee for their permission to use their "Entry to the Real World" article as a base for the "The Crucial First Year" chapter.

All those employers, career educators and recent graduates who shared their thoughts and invaluable experiences.

Table of Contents

Author's Notes

1. The following "job search terms" have been used interchangeably throughout the book:
    i)   Interviewer (s) has been used in the singular and plural form.
    ii) He, she and they.
    iii) Hirers, interviewers, recruiters and employers.
    iv) CACEE and ACCIS, because it will still be some time before those involved in on-campus recruiting make the transition.
    v)   Organizations, companies and firms. Not wanting to steer your thoughts in a particular direction these words were used randomly throughout the book. Use the appropriate word which applies to you and fits your particular area of interest.
    vi) I have called the career services offered by your universities and colleges "Career Centres". If your institution refers to it by another name, use "it" each time you see the term "Career Centre".

2. A survey was conducted of recent graduates, career educators and employers. The survey is discussed in detail in Chapters 9, 10 and 11, but often referred to before then.

3. The sample cover letters, resumes, CACEE forms and interview follow up letters are only given as style and format guidelines. As I have discussed throughout this book, without doing in-depth research into both the job and the organization and tailoring your correspondence to their needs, it is impossible to "make" samples "content-perfect". Don't ever copy anyone's letters or resumes. Use samples as a guide but make sure each piece of collateral has your distinctive mark.

Why You Need to Read This Book

1

Over the past six months I have been asked the same question: "Why are you writing the book?" I'll share with you the answer I gave to all my friends. It will explain why you need to read this book.

Every summer for the past fourteen years, I have had an endless stream of visitors. Not my family and friends coming to enjoy the "joie de vivre" of Montreal, but a never ending line-up of Davids, Patricias, Jeans, Wendys and Tonys in search of the job search guide for the real world. They were the children, relatives or friends of my hairdresser, my banker, my lawyer, my baker, my tailor, my dry cleaner or my Partners. They knew my wife, or her hairdresser, banker, lawyer, tailor, dry cleaner or Partners. (I was thankful that my wife and I shared our baker.)

Then there were those who had some connection to my father-in-law or his wide circle of friends, or they knew somebody who worked at my firm or at least their hairdresser, banker, lawyer, baker, tailor, dry cleaner or Partner did. One person just happened to have Expos season tickets in the same section as me and that was connection enough.

I always admired their tenacity and I gave them high marks for their ability to network. I gave them a failing grade, however, for being eight months late.

The final proof that I was doing the right thing in writing this book came after I had (almost) finished the first draft.

The son of a very dear friend, whom I will call Sid because that is his name, started to look for a job a week before his final class of his graduating semester. He was one of the fortunate ones. He was able to stay on and work full time at the part time job he had held throughout his three years at school. He was lucky – unlike my annual summer visitors, he was only under-employed not unemployed.

The more that you read,
the more things you will know.
The more that you learn,
the more places you'll go.
You might learn
a way to earn a
few dollars.

Dr. Seuss

Most of my visitors were in a confused state and offered one or more of the following excuses for being in their predicament:

They did not know "on-campus recruiting" existed.

They thought they could wait until after graduation when they would have more time.

They really did not know what they wanted to do.

They thought they might go to Law School or do an MBA.

They were considering taking the year off and travelling the world.

They wanted to take the summer off and were afraid an employer would want them to start work right away.

They did not realize that organizations hired that far in advance.

They had heard that there was a Career Centre at their school but they were not sure where it was.

They were hoping one of their parents' friends would hire them.

They did not think their marks were good enough to get a job.

I have addressed every one of these issues in this book. And many more. Can I guarantee that you will have a job when you graduate if you follow all the advice in this book? No. But what I can assure you is that if you follow the guidance, you will be way ahead of your competition. If you work hard at getting a job, treat it as a must-pass course, and you are resolute in the pursuit of your goals, your self confidence will soar. Once that is achieved, your ability to network will improve immeasurably and your new found poise and increased sense of self-worth will permeate everything you do to secure a job.

The Outlook

The National Unemployment rate stood at 9.5% in June, 1995.

In 1996 over 200,000 students are due to graduate from university and college in Canada, and over 2,000,000 in the USA.

Employers are operating with smaller staffs and are becoming more demanding in their qualification requirements, as well as more selective in their hiring.

This is far from encouraging news if you are one of these graduates, but there are still thousands of excellent entry level jobs available. This book

Networking is a necessity in order to tap the "hidden-job market" which contains in excess of 80% of the available jobs in the country. The labour market of the 90s lends itself to the networking process since the supply of labour far exceeds the demand and employers are reluctant to publicize their vacancies knowing that the response will be overwhelming.

Ernie Hovell
Director, Career Planning &
Employment Centre,
Acadia University

will provide you with insight into how today's job market operates and what recruiters really want. Follow all the advice and you will have a job when you graduate.

Recruiting Pearls of Wisdom

1. You have to start the job search process immediately. If you haven't already started, today is the day.

2. Having practical computer skills is essential regardless of your field of interest. You must have, not only the current skills, but the desire and ability to constantly update and perfect those skills.

3. Accept the premise that the most qualified applicant does not necessarily get the job. It is usually the person who best understands the rules of the recruiting game and who plays it well.

4. You must do extensive research on the organizations in which you are interested. Not only the facts and figures, but their philosophies, mission statements, and future plans. Your research on the interviewers and recruiters should include their systems and styles, their likes and dislikes.

5. Be yourself. The short term satisfaction of landing a job because you pretended to have the qualities for the position will ultimately lead to long term dissatisfaction and disappointment.

6. In every situation, try to capitalize on your strengths, your relevant experiences and what makes you special. Emphasize them whenever you have the opportunity throughout the job hunt process.

7. Remember that charm and warmth will get you a lot further than rudeness and aggression. Whether you are persuading a network contact to give you thirty minutes of his or her time or trying to get through that "tough-as-nails" secretary, charm and a smile will work wonders.

8. Think constantly about the particular demands of the position and what the recruiters want. Don't use this knowledge to become someone else, use it to decide if you really want that job and if you want to work for that organization.

The toughest part of getting a job was balancing school, extra-curricular activities, working and concentrating on doing well with interviews, during the fall semester.

A. Scott Walker
Residential Sales Representative,
Union Gas Ltd.,
Wilfrid Laurier University Grad '94

13

9. Never forget that recruiters love to hire people they like and with whom they feel comfortable. If they think you will fit in and will ultimately make them look good, chances are they will hire you.

10. The days of employment for life appear to be over. When you select your first employer, you can no longer think of it as being your only one. Think of it as being the stepping stone to the rest of your career. It is usually the strength of your first job that gets you the second. And from the second, the third. Careers and resumes are built over long periods of time. The stronger the foundation, the more stable the building.

11. Remember that you will be judged on everything you do and say throughout the recruiting process, not just at the formal events. They will judge your cover letter, your resume, your thank-you letter, your answering machine and your friends. They will assess your references, your handshake, your physical appearance, your voice and your table manners. They will test your ability to think, analyse, assess and research. They will appraise your communication skills every step of the way.

12. You will have to provide the impetus to make things happen. Attend all the seminars offered, make the calls, write the letters and follow up on applications and networking contacts. No one is going to do it for you.

13. Keep in mind as you meet recruiters what general qualities they are looking for in the candidates they would like to hire:

    Flexibility Your willingness to do a wide variety of different tasks, be a part of a broad range of groups and teams, and work for different people.

    Manageability Your ability and desire to be trained, managed and supervised.

    Adaptability Your aptitude to learn about new environments, techniques and systems and accept the new challenges facing you in the workplace.

    Self Confidence Your facility to meet new people, as well as interact with all levels of staff, with poise and diplomacy, without being arrogant or impolite.

14. You must look upon your search for a job as an integral part of your graduating year. It is not something that you can work on in your spare time. It must be built into your schedule. Think of it as a compulsory course you must take.

The jobs are there and people get hired every day. There is just much more competition.

Maria Borg-Olivier
Co-operative Education
Coordinator, Seneca College

Commit the same amount of energy to yourself and your career pursuits as you would to your academic courses. Don't make yourself second priority.

Jan Basso
Director, Co-operative Education
& Career Services,
Wilfrid Laurier University

14

15. The kind of effort it takes to get a job is the same effort you should assure recruiters you will put into your first, on-the-job assignment.

16. Recognize that you are going to be nervous throughout the process, particularly as you get closer to landing the "big job". This is perfectly normal. Use it to boost your energy level and your drive to succeed.

17. Use your contacts wherever and whenever you can but remember, they might be good enough to get you an interview, but seldom a job. That you will have to get yourself.

18. You are going to have to be relentless in the pursuit of your goals. You will get rejection letters, doors will be shut in your face and people will refuse to meet you. Don't let it get you down; it's all part of the process. Make sure you didn't do anything wrong and then move on to the next chapter.

19. At the end of each interview ask yourself two questions:

> Did they see the real me?
> Did I do my best?

If the answer to both questions is yes, be proud of yourself whatever the outcome. If the answer is no, ask yourself what you can do to improve your performance.

20. You cannot overestimate the importance of a handshake. As evidence of the way I feel, I am giving it prominence in this key section to make sure you don't miss it. Your manner should be the same no matter whose hand you are shaking. Look the person in the eye and shake their right hand firmly with your right hand. Never bone-crushing or jelly-fish limp, shake firmly and with confidence. Some people will evaluate your entire personality based on your handshake. Make sure they only see you as self-assured and poised.

21. If you sent an application to an organization through their on-campus recruiting campaign and you are not selected for an interview, it's OK to be disappointed but you should not give up hope. Wait a couple of weeks, then send a cover letter and your resume. You have nothing to lose. You never know who may review your application this time. The result could be different.

22. Do not try to read anything into the rejection letters you receive. They are usually form letters.

Before the recruitment process started, I was told that very few people would get jobs. There are very few jobs available and only the top academic students get offers. By the time the process ended, I had interviewed with 10 companies, I had been offered and had accepted the position I wanted, and I was not one of the top academic students. The recruitment process does work!

A. Scott Walker
Residential Sales Representative,
Union Gas Ltd.,
Wilfrid Laurier University Grad '94

Far too many people spend time analysing the letter rather than analysing why they didn't get the job. My advice is that you contact the company to find out why you were not selected. Try to speak to the decision maker, the person who reviewed the resumes or the person who interviewed you. Be polite, ask for help and explain that you would like to improve your performance and that is why you are phoning to ask for advice. It is not the time to ask for a second chance. Just let them know that if their situation does change, you are still interested in them. Let your self confidence and professionalism shine through.

23. Do not ever chew gum. I wasn't going to mention this because it seemed so obvious but when two of the last three people I interviewed entered the room chewing gum, I felt compelled to include these five words. Do not ever chew gum.

24. Remember that the organization will be spending thousands of dollars training you in the first six months on the job. Throughout the process, keep in mind that you have to convince everyone involved in the recruiting process that you are worth the expense.

The Crucial Sixty Seconds

As the well-known shampoo commercial says "You never get a second chance to make a first impression" and first impressions are crucial in the job hunt. Sixty seconds are all you have to impress people throughout the recruiting process. Every step of the way, they'll be forming instant opinions about you.

Meeting someone for the first time

Whether it is at a Career Fair, a cocktail party, luncheon, company information session or just prior to the interview, whatever you do, or say, and how you look, will effect a potential employer's opinion of you. If they are initially impressed, you'll have to do something really negative to change how they feel about you. Conversely, if you do not impress them at the first meeting, you are going to have to perform exceptionally to alter their view. But will you get another opportunity?

Make that first impression count; from the firm handshake right down to the polished shoes!

Jocelyne Younan
Director, MBA Career Centre,
McGill University

Cover letters

Whether you are sending an unsolicited resume to an organization or replying to an advertisement, your cover letter is going to be the key in persuading the reader to read your resume. Keep in mind that the recruiter will spend about sixty seconds scanning it. If they are impressed they'll generally read it again. If not, your cover letter and unread resume will be put in the "Thanks, but no thanks" file. If they begin to read your resume, you have your foot in the door.

Resumes

Once your resume is complete, take two steps back and ask yourself one question: would you want to read it? When you first meet someone, his or her first impression of you is based solely on what you look like and your handshake. Well, your resume is much the same – it makes that all-important first impression based on appearance, not content. Make sure it's something of which you are proud.

On the phone

When speaking on the phone, it is essential that you rehearse what you are going to say. The person to whom you are speaking cannot see you and might easily be distracted by other work. It is crucial that you make an immediate impression, that you are able to grab and keep their attention. Keep in mind how easy it is for them to refuse to be of assistance.

Learning how to look for and secure a job is the most critical life skill we can acquire.

Jennifer Young
Chair, Department of Co-operative Education, The University College of the Cariboo

The Approach to Your Job Search

2

Career Centres

For your job search to be truly effective, you should be intimately familiar with the services your university or college career centre provides and be prepared for it to become your "home-away-from-home" during your entire campaign. If you are fortunate enough to be at an institution that has more than one career centre, take advantage. Get to know them all. Make sure you know what's happening at both centres and keep in touch. It's the most important resource in your job search and offers a great deal of assistance to both current students and recent grads.

Career exploration and guidance

I will not be covering this subject in any detail in this book primarily because I believe it is not a topic that can be effectively dealt with by simply reading a book and filling in charts.

If you are at the stage of your life where you have chosen your career path and you're happy with your decision, go ahead and pursue your dream. If not, my advice to you is to immediately seek professional career counselling. Most of your institutions provide this service. Take advantage of it. Trained counsellors will be able to assist you in exploring the myriad of opportunities available, once they've helped you in uncovering your motivations, goals, skills and interests. I strongly suggest that you complement this advice by having discussions with both experienced professionals and recent graduates in the fields you are considering. I have discussed the most effective ways of doing this in the chapter on networking.

Only those who dare to fail greatly can ever achieve greatly.

Robert F. Kennedy

Career planning

Through experienced career counsellors, your Career Centre will lead you to examine interests, skills, values, motivations, goals and opportunities. This should be the starting point of your decision-making process.

They will use a variety of methods to assist you in the assessment stage including personal interviews, psychological testing and computer exploration programs. Occupation alternatives will be identified and explored. They'll help you to research these alternatives and identify employment opportunities.

Career information

They provide comprehensive resource material in print, video and audio formats on careers, employers, job search techniques and further educational opportunities. They are usually able to provide you with comprehensive labour market information.

Job search assistance

The Centre's overall mandate is to provide assistance in preparing you for the job search process. Many offer workshops and counselling sessions on resume preparation, interview techniques, career planning and other job search tactics. These are conducted by both on-staff counsellors and by on-campus employers brought in by the Centre to provide students with the opportunity to learn, first hand, from those recruiting on campus. The on-campus recruiting world is small. Seasoned recruiters and career centre personnel know each other well and, as a result, a great deal of informal recruiting activity takes place. You can take advantage of this if the career centre professionals get to know you well.

Graduate study information

Often, the Centre will provide information with respect to admission test applications, professional school fact sheets and applications for Government positions.

On-campus recruiting

The Centre provides all the essential services business, industry, government and social agencies need to enable them to effectively and efficiently

Do the homework... job search takes time, patience and hard work, but pays off.

Joy Mitchell
Employment Services Coordinator,
Wilfrid Laurier University

20

interview and recruit students. This includes advice on all aspects of student hiring and the coordination of the collection, review and selection of resumes as well as the scheduling of interviews.

Job posting service

Summer, part-time and permanent jobs are usually posted at the Centre and other strategic locations across campus. Another reason to visit the Centre is to ensure that you don't miss any postings or deadlines.

'Career Options' magazine

This magazine is published annually by the Canadian Association of Career Educators and Employers (CACEE) free of charge. It is available at most Career Centres. It provides information on current career and employment issues, sample resumes, cover letters and information on companies that often recruit on Canadian campuses.

Special events

The Centre will be able to provide you with all the relevant information about events taking place that concern your job search. Career Fairs, company information sessions, industry or organization sponsored meetings, lunches, cocktail parties or receptions are usually co-ordinated and publicized through the Centre. Many of these events take place immediately after classes begin in the Fall so make sure you visit the Centre as soon as you can.

Effective use of the services of the Career Centre

As mentioned, the first step is to get to know the people and to know your way around the Centre. If they provide tours of the facility take one. If you are so inclined volunteer at the Centre. It's a great way to get to know the people there and to have regular and easier access to the latest information. With recent budget cuts I am sure they will appreciate your efforts, and you'll have the inside track on new job opportunities.

Attend a workshop on how to complete a resume. If you learn even one thing, it may just be what makes the difference.

Doreen Knol
Manager, Engineering Career
Services, McMaster University

Newspaper Advertisements

Newspaper 'career' ads may prove to be a futile search for a job, but they can be a useful tool. You need to understand certain aspects of why companies place ads, what your chances are, and how to most effectively use your job search skills when answering an ad.

Timing

Most organizations advertise through the media when they have an immediate opening. Obviously, if it is the Fall and you are graduating in the Spring, these may appear to be of no use to you. If you are graduating in December, they may be more useful to you but only if the potential employer can wait for you for what may be up to a few months. Are these advertisements therefore only of use to you when you're just about to graduate? Yes, but there is a potential hidden market lurking below the surface that you should not ignore.

The approach

First, I will deal with the advertisements that fit into your time frame, and then I'll address the hidden market. It's essential that you read every newspaper available in the geographic area in which you are interested as well as the national newspapers. I recommend two publications: The National Edition of the Globe and Mail and the Canadian Employment Weekly. This may seem like an expensive proposition but most newspapers are usually available at the school library, the local library and your career centre. The moment you spot an advertisement that interests you, react immediately and follow the steps I've outlined in the chapters on cover letters and resumes.

The best advice I can give you with respect to this part of your campaign is – don't become discouraged. You will often go days, even weeks, without seeing an advertisement that interests you or for which you are qualified. What will frustrate you even more will be the fact that you will constantly see advertisements for great positions in your field, if only you had a few years of experience. This fact should encourage rather than disappoint you. It will mean a few things. First, that your field of interest is currently hiring, which is always a good sign. Second, it will provide you with a key piece of research information. You now have in your possession the name of the

Never, never, never give up looking for a job. Always try to stay positive especially when things look "bleak."

George Clapham
Director, Co-operative Education
& Placement, Centennial College

person to whom you can address your unsolicited resume. Make sure you write down the name, position and address in each case. It will serve to lessen your frustration later and, having one new contact, you can proceed with renewed enthusiasm.

The hidden market

For those of you for whom the timing is wrong there is a vital, two-pronged approach to newspaper advertisements. Even though I said earlier that if it is September and you are graduating in the Spring, there is little chance of getting a job through the newspaper, it is essential that you read the newspapers regularly to build up your contact base. Begin immediately to record every name and address in your area of interest. Armed with this information, you can proceed in two ways. If the organization is advertising for a specific entry level position for which you will be qualified when you graduate, apply anyway.

Organizations will generally react by either telling you they cannot wait until Spring but will keep your application on file, or that they simply do not keep resumes on file. In the first scenario, you have your foot in the door. As time comes closer to graduation, you can follow up with a letter and phone call to the contact person, clearly referring to your earlier application, and inquire if a position has become available.

If the organization is very impressed with your application they may want to see you immediately, even if you're not available to fill their current vacancy. I know of several such cases. A student recently told me her story: a company interviewed her because they were very impressed with her cover letter and resume, even though they knew she wouldn't be available for another six months. Four months after the first interview, another entry-level position became available and this time, rather than advertise, they contacted her and offered her the position. She even worked part time for them until she graduated.

Networking

It is often said in recruiting and employment circles that the best jobs are never advertised. If this is true (and I have never seen a statistic to support or

Visit and talk with as many people as possible regarding potential job opportunities; this includes friends, family, neighbours, friends of the family, etc. – jobs come from many, many contacts.

Alex Gallacher
Manager, Human Resources,
Mintz & Partners

Develop networking skills so they become part of who you are – 'second nature'.

Doreen Knol
Manager, Engineering Career
Services, McMaster University

23

Your industry contacts are important... not all companies hire through school channels.

Bryce Cooper
Mechanical Engineer,
PanCanadian Petroleum Limited,
McGill University Grad '95

Join the school club of the career in which you are interested. They host events where you can meet employees of firms you may want to work for. Sometimes, the interviewer will be at these social events and may remember familiar faces during the interview.

Corrina Debusschere
Intermediate Accountant,
Mintz & Partners,
Wilfrid Laurier University Grad '94

to refute this), how do you become aware of this market and more importantly, how do you access it?

Most students lament the fact that they don't have contacts and thus the hidden job market is closed to them. It may seem that way, but I think you'll be amazed how many more people you have in your network than you realize.

The following is a list that will serve to jog your brain to uncover your potential network:

The "obvious" Your parents; your family

The "fairly obvious" Your parents' friends; your family's friends; your friends' parents; your friends' family

The "not-so-obvious" Your professors; your family bank manager, doctor, lawyer, notary and accountant; your high school, college and CEGEP teachers; members of your clergy; your parents' business associates; people for whom you have worked; professional associations related to your areas of interest; your schools' alumni associations

The "much-less-obvious" Your neighbours; people you have met in your community; recent graduates who were successful in their job search; your sports coaches; your family real estate agent; the manager of your favourite restaurant; people you may have met through internships, job shadow programs and work terms; your friends' friends; your friends' friends' family

The secret to succeeding in uncovering your network is to ask each of the people mentioned above who they know in your field, and if they are willing to refer you. The second step is to ask each of these people if they know anyone who may know someone you could contact who may be of assistance and so on and so on. People's initial response is usually that they do not know anyone. Be persistent, give them some time to think about it, and get back to them. Thank each person for their help and encourage them to let you know if they think of any additional people.

Tell the world you're looking

People who are looking for a job generally do not broadcast the fact. This is either because they are out of a job and are too embarrassed to tell anyone or they are currently employed and can't risk their current employer finding out they are looking around. As a graduating student, you will not be faced with the latter dilemma unless you have a part-time job. If this is your situation, I strongly suggest you tell your part-time employer you are looking for full-time employment, then discuss those employment possibilities. Do this as soon as possible. Potential employers will undoubtedly want to contact your current employer for references which makes it essential that they are aware of your campaign. In addition, if you are keen to work full time for your current employer after graduation, the sooner you can secure a position the better. It will save both you and the organization the time and money associated with going through the recruiting process.

Information and contact networking

Your key tool for meeting your networking contacts is your telephone. It is essential that your approach be professional, upbeat, warm and friendly. You should display a high energy level and know what you are going to say.

When you have a contact

In these situations, the purpose of the call is to arrange a meeting and not to give your network contact all the information on the phone. Meeting the person face-to-face is crucial and will be far more effective, so make the scheduling of the meeting the objective of each call. Make the calls brief and ask for a half hour of their time. Almost everyone can spare half an hour, especially if you're flexible as to the time of the meeting. You have to be. Remember, they are doing you a favour so you have to have the meeting at a time that is most convenient to them. If you are being referred to the person you are calling by someone else, mention the name of your referral immediately when you call. It will usually ensure you get through the "administrative barriers" that are often put up around senior management.

When you don't have a contact

This is far more difficult. Your best bet is to call a company and tell them you're exploring opportunities with organizations in their field and you

The more people you know, the better you will do your job.

Mike Tuff
Coordinator
Education & Training,
The Toronto-Dominion Bank

Always be networking. The 90 year old lady you help on the bus could be Paul Desmarais' mom.

Scott Gregory
Manager of Career Services,
Faculty of Administration,
University of Ottawa

would like to meet with someone for fifteen minutes to get some information on the industry and the organization. Don't tell them you are looking for a job and don't ask for an interview. Just ask for information about the company and any opportunities that the person you meet may know of in the field. If they are impressed with you, you will be pleased with their reaction. Be positive, upbeat, energetic and charming.

Follow up the meeting with a thank-you letter and if you are interested in the company, a copy of your resume, of course. You now have your foot in the door. Seize the opportunity.

If you have the name of a person to call, but do not have a name of a contact to mention, the best time to call is before 8:30 am, after 5:00 pm or at lunch time. The "administrative barriers" are likely to be less formidable at these times and your chances of actually speaking to the person are therefore much greater.

Networking doesn't have to be a scary thing – develop your own style of networking that you are comfortable with.

Rebecca Burwell
Career Counsellor, Seneca College

Rehearsal

If you are nervous making these calls, develop a script and practice it before each call. Don't get into the habit of reading it, though. It will sound stilted and won't allow your warmth and personality to shine through.

Network database

From the moment you start your job search, you should keep a database of your network contacts. They should contain the name, address, phone and fax numbers of each contact, as well as the name of your referral source if there is one. Many students effectively use contacts' business cards as the starting point for their database.

Researching Organizations, Professions and Industries

Every recruiter surveyed agreed that an essential aspect of the job search process was the need to do extensive research of organizations at every stage of the recruiting process. I am convinced that the more you know about the world that you are thinking of entering, the wiser you will be. With such a crucial decision pending in the very near future, the more you are able to learn about an organization, profession or industry the more sound will be your final choice.

Throughout the book I have referred to the value of your research and how you will use the information at every stage of your campaign. The two primary reasons for doing research are to develop a list of potential employers to whom you can apply and to learn as much as possible about specific employers in whom you are interested.

Developing a list of employers

Your institution's Career Centre and libraries will undoubtedly be the best places for you to begin your search. You will be astounded by the number of reference sources available. If you have never undertaken this type of research before, it is best to ask the reference librarian for assistance.

The Directory of Canadian Associations is an essential referral source of organizations in your particular field. This publication provides the names, addresses, telephone and fax numbers of all associations in Canada. By contacting the pertinent associations, you will be able to get a listing of the members, as well as copies of their newsletters, magazines and literature. They will often be able to furnish you with information concerning association meetings, and possibly even job openings. While associations' attitudes on giving out this information vary tremendously, my advice is that you be as charming and polite as possible and you will be amazed at how successful you can be. The following is a list of other important sources for your general research:

Canadian Key Business Directory
Supplies a listing of all major businesses in Canada.

Canadian Advertising Rates and Data
They will provide you with an index of major advertisers and advertising agencies.

Writers' Market
Gives a list of magazines, newspapers and publishing houses in Canada.

Community and Social Service Directory
Furnishes an inventory of books and reports on industries and companies.

Networking is the foundation of all looking-for-work endeavours. The more people you meet and who are aware of what you have to offer, the more chance you have of finding the type of work you want. Networking creates opportunity!

Marilyn Van Norman
Director, Career Centre,
University of Toronto

Networking means building and maintaining a pool of contacts who will endorse you as a good candidate for employment. Never leave any stone unturned.

Jill Curley
Career Placement Counsellor,
Mount Saint Vincent University

Keep in touch with friends. They might be able to alert you to job openings in their companies that might be of interest to you.

Debbie Ng
Software Designer,
Unisys GSG Canada Inc.,
McGill University Grad '94

Dun and Bradstreet
Publishes a number of books and reports on industries and companies.

Financial Post Annual Survey
This publication produces a report on the largest organizations, businesses and firms in Canada in a wide variety of industries and categories and classifications.

Fraser's Canadian Trade Directory
Is a listing of all Canadian suppliers or manufacturers (including addresses and how to get their catalogues).

The Blue Book of Canadian Business
This publication analyses 130 of the major Canadian companies each year including a report on their strengths and weaknesses.

The Business Opportunity Sourcing System (B.O.S.S.)
This is a Federal Government publication which will give you up to date data on a wide variety of industries.

For those of you searching for jobs in the Consulting, Accounting, Finance, Manufacturing, Sales, Marketing, Non-Profit or High Tech industries, you may find the following books helpful:

Consulting

Canadian Environmental Directory
Included, among others, is a catalogue of related organizations, government agencies, and a directory of products and services.

Environmental Resource Book
A Canadian directory of environmental information such as environmental protection and organizations providing information services.

Directory of Canadian Management Consultants
A registry of Consulting firms and essential details about them.

28

Accounting, finance and manufacturing

The Toronto Stock Exchange Review
A monthly review containing statistical reports and information about dividends, stock, options and futures. It also has information about newly listed companies.

Directory of Members of the Trust Companies Association of Canada

The Canadian Association of Financial Planners

Directory of Canadian Chartered Accountants
Provides a list of names and addresses of all Canadian Chartered Accountants.

Canadian Trade Index
An inventory, by trade, of all major Canadian organizations.

Scott's Industrial Directory
A register of Canadian manufacturers in each community and by product classification. (Also available on computer disk called *"Scott's Selectory"*)

Sales and marketing

The National List of Advertisers
A directory of advertisers, advertising agencies' addresses and their largest accounts.

Marketing research organizations

Canadian Advertising Rates and Data (CARD Directory)
Will give you the names and addresses of all Canadian community newspapers, daily newspapers and radio stations.

ACTA Directory (Alliance of Canadian Travel Association)
A catalogue of the Canadian representatives of travel wholesalers, hotels, tourist offices, car rental agencies of foreign countries.

Hotel & Travel Index
Directory of hotels in Canada, the United States and some countries overseas.

It always helps to get your foot in the door through an established contact. If you are reluctant to do so, keep in mind that others are not.

Tina Cerulli
Systems Analyst,
CP Rail System,
McGill University Grad '94

Non-profit

Directory of Canadian Museums
A registry of museum associations, related organizations and museums in Canada.

Canadian Hospital Directory
A directory of all Canadian hospitals.

High Tech

The CATAlog (Canadian Advanced Technology Association)
A corporate directory of a cross section of the Canadian Advanced Technology Association member companies and organizations. It also outlines their products, services and qualifications.

Other sources
Newspaper advertisements, business related articles and the Yellow Pages are very good places to uncover information about smaller local organizations and businesses in your area. As you scan the media, try to look beyond the news for other possible leads on uncovering organizations that may be recruiting in your field. Be on the lookout for:

New business openings
Business expansions
Takeovers
Companies that have landed large contracts
Companies that are moving to your area
Organizations that have purchased land or buildings

Researching individual organizations
You ultimately have to answer one question: "If I was offered a job, would I want to work for this organization?" This is the reason you do in-depth research on each organization in which you are interested. Before you get to this stage, however, you must decide whether an organization is worthy of receiving your resume or CACEE form. Without a doubt, you will acquire very useful information from the organization throughout the recruiting process. Keep in mind that this is disseminated as part of the organization's

The toughest part of getting a job was getting information on the available companies in a broad sense, for example, all companies involved in telecommunications research in Canada.

Gerald Boersma
Software Engineer,
MPR Teltech Ltd.,
Carleton University Grad '95

sales pitch to persuade you and your classmates to work for them. You need to get as much objective information as possible, both factual and personal opinion because you will need this information to make your decision, and because most organizations will also view your level of knowledge about them as a sign of real interest and enthusiasm.

You should also read all the most recent literature available on the organization in which you are interested. Your best source is your library. Your library will probably have a CD ROM system where you might locate articles on a particular organization simply by entering the name of the company. Once you have a list of articles, you must find out if your particular library carries these publications or periodicals. If they do not, call all the libraries in your area in order to locate one that does carry the periodicals you need. Some articles may just inform you about the company's current events. This is useful for "small talk" with company representatives or to give you an idea of a company's involvement in everything from charity events to lawsuits. During the recruiting process, this always left a significant, positive impression on me.

Let's examine what's important for you to know about each organization in your field:

Is it a corporation, partnership, joint venture, government agency, or non-profit organization?
If it is a corporation, is it private or public?
If it is a public corporation, are its shares listed on a stock exchange? Which one?
If it is a private company, who are the shareholders?
Is it a branch, division or subsidiary of another company?
What exactly does the organization do?
What products or services does it provide?
Does it manufacture, import, construct or develop?
How long has it been in operation?
Where are the operations located?
How many people are currently employed?
How many at each location?
What is the management structure?

Research is a key element in job search success! Information about the job description, employer and industry will help you to tailor your answers in an interview more effectively, prepare a more focused resume, express how your skills and interests contribute to the employer's goals and assist you in conducting a targeted job search that meets your career objectives.

Ann-Marie Elliott
Placement Services Coordinator,
York University

Research
Before writing the cover letter
Before the first interview
Before the second interview
Before accepting the job offer.

Jocelyne Younan
Director, MBA Career Centre,
McGill University

Remember, the research is for your benefit – the time taken to find out about a company indicates enthusiasm and initiative, it allows you to compare your own interests and goals with that of the company and provides a common base to ask and answer questions in your interview.

Jill Curley
Career Placement Counsellor,
Mount Saint Vincent University

What is the predominant management philosophy and style?
Who are the key players in the organization?
Have there been any recent major changes in the senior management of the organization?
Is the company experiencing periods of growth or slowdown?
Are there plans for expansion?
Are there plans for cutbacks and retrenchment?
Are new major products, services or technological changes planned?
What is the organization's market position?
What is the current financial state of the organization?
What types of positions are available?
What are your chances of promotion?

If your research resulted in positive answers to most of these questions, you can feel free to apply, knowing that this seems like the type of organization for which you would like to work. Once you seem close to receiving a job offer, you must then contemplate a new set of criteria to determine whether this organization is the place where you would actually like to begin your career.

Establishing criteria

Here is a list of points you should be considering and discussing as you meet with recruiters, managers and staff. Discuss each of these with as many people as possible to obtain different points of view. You should also contact your career centre to obtain referrals from alumni who may now be working for the organization.

The corporate climate
Working conditions
The type of work you will be doing
Training programs
Evaluation system
Salary and benefits (insurance, vacation time, etc.)
The people you would be working with each day
Geographical location
Level of responsibility

Potential for learning new skills
Job security

With the answer to these questions and with the help of the worksheet at the end of the chapter on assessing offers, you should be in a very good position to decide which of the many job offers you would like to accept.

Job Search Events

3

In this chapter I will cover the six most common events that usually take place fairly early in the recruiting year: Career Fairs, Job Fairs, cocktail parties, breakfasts, luncheons and dinners and Organization Information Sessions.

Each of these events provides an excellent opportunity to meet employers. Once you have met them, each subsequent event gives you an occasion to solidify your relationship with those recruiters you have previously met and the chance to meet more of those whom you have not.

Career Fairs

There exists a direct correlation between the preparation and the effort you put into a Career Fair and how much you will benefit from them. Undoubtedly, the more effort you invest the more you will benefit from the experience.

Career Fairs are also called Career Days and Career Exploration Days. They should not be confused with Job Fairs which I will cover later in the chapter. The objectives of a Fair are to provide an opportunity for you to meet with organizations who are looking to hire on campus and for the recruiters to meet potential candidates as well as to provide them with information concerning their organization and industry.

I know many people who have gotten asked to first interviews and jobs after meeting the people from the career fairs.

Dawn Ursuliak
Risk Management Analyst,
TransAlta Utilities Corporation,
University of Alberta Grad '93

The wrong approach

Over the years I've seen so many students enter a Career Fair, proceed to walk the entire length of the site and leave in under three minutes having decided there were no jobs for them. The slightly more ambitious walk through the exhibit, pick up brochures wherever they are sure they can avoid getting into a conversation with an organization's representative and then leave. This longer process may take fifteen minutes. Both are a total waste of time.

The right approach

Career Days are the best opportunity for you to network, talk to professionals in the field and obtain invaluable information very early in the job search process. Best of all, it can be done in a fairly informal setting where you can ask most of your questions and have very little formally expected of you.

Early preparation

Have business cards made. These days you can have a set of business cards printed for under $20, a very small outlay for a long term investment. The card should include your name, address and all your contact phone numbers.

Try to find out, as soon as possible, which organizations will be attending the event. A detailed list will be available, long before the fair, from the organizers. Ask them for the list. If they are reluctant to provide you with it, volunteer to work on the event. They will welcome the help. You will not only have early access to the list of attendees but an automatic introduction to the organizations' representatives on the day of the event.

Do your company research immediately. This research enables you to divide exhibitors into two basic categories, those you are interested in and those you are not. This will ensure that you immediately start to acquire knowledge about the companies in which you are interested and on which you will focus. This knowledge of the organization will enable you to begin to prepare meaningful questions. Nothing irritates a recruiter more than being asked "who are you and what does your company do". Conversely, nothing impresses them more than a student with a basic understanding of their organization, its products and industry. In addition, the Career Fair is an excellent opportunity to make a good first impression. The more knowledge you have the more likely you are to impress.

The event

Dress well but don't dress as if you are going to an interview. It will look like you are trying too hard to impress. Dress neatly and conservatively. Even though it is far more difficult and takes far more initial courage, it is advisable to walk around by yourself. If you are with a group of students, you will likely be distracted from your game plan and your priorities.

Arrange your day so that you can devote sufficient time to the Career Fair. Do not simply make it a rushed visit between classes.

There are risks and costs to a program of action. But they are far less than the long range risks and costs of comfortable inaction.

John F. Kennedy

Attend career fairs with an open mind. Be prepared to look at each and every company as a potential opportunity.

Gloria J. Majich
Employment Supervisor,
Babcock & Wilcox

36

As soon as you arrive, check the list of attendees. There are often last minute additions. Participating organizations usually provide a brief profile which should enable you to classify them as you did with those on your original list. If you do not have enough information to classify them, you may want to stop by and visit anyway if you have time.

Once you have adjusted your original list to include any of the late additions, take the total time you plan to spend at the Career Day, deduct twenty minutes and divide by the number of companies you want to visit. You now have an idea of how much time you have to spend on each employer less a couple of minutes. The "special twenty minutes" will be used to re-visit those employers who particularly impress you. You are now ready to visit the potential employers!

Visiting the employers

Be warm and friendly and self confident. Approach a representative, extend your hand and introduce yourself "Hello, my name is John Smith. I am a graduating student and am interested in finding out more about your company and the opportunities it currently has to offer graduates". Hand over your business card. Undoubtedly, they will be impressed. You may want to add that you had the cards prepared for the recruiting process to make it easier for employers to remember you and contact you.

A sharp recruiter may ask you at this stage what you know about their organization so be prepared. This is where not having done your research hurts but if you were genuinely unable to find any research source don't hesitate to say so.

You now have the opportunity to ask all your questions. Your objective is obviously to find out as much about the organization and its people as you can. You may want to ask:

"What are you looking for when you hire new graduates?"
"What training is offered?"
"What is a typical career path?"
"How many graduates are you hiring?"

Organizations usually send their most dynamic, outgoing people so this should be more than enough to get them talking about their organization and

After applying for the same position within a one week span, I received two letters: one saying "thanks but no thanks", the other requesting that I come for an interview. I used the same resume, same cover letter. The difference was a business card given to me at a job fair – it led to my current position. Had I not taken the time to meet the gentleman from the company, I might still be job hunting today.

Jim Fridfinnson
Customer Service Officer,
The Toronto-Dominion Bank,
Southern Alberta Institute of
Technology Grad '92

Research the organization in which you have an interest, prior to attending a career fair. Go to the fair, prepared to ask questions and make a positive impression.

Marilyn Van Norman
Director, Career Centre,
University of Toronto

their careers. If in your research, you uncovered pertinent information with respect to the organization that could have an effect on recruiting, you may also want to ask about it. For example, "I read in the newspaper that you are opening a new plant in Newtown. How will this impact your recruiting needs for this year?"

Many organizations have equal opportunity employment (equity) programs in place. If you belong to one of the designated groups, it may be to your benefit to inquire about these opportunities at this stage and let them know that they are applicable to you.

Be prepared to answer some basic questions. These should generally be no more complex than inquiries about your degree, your career aspirations and possibly your desired job location.

If you are impressed, stick around for a while. Try to find out if any of the people attending are actually going to be doing the interviews. It is never too early to establish a rapport and to make sure they remember you.

Ensure that you obtain all the literature you don't already have. For the literature you do have, do not be shy to say you do, it certainly will not hurt to show you have done your homework.

Do not, under any circumstances, overstay your welcome or your allotment of time. Remember, you will need a few minutes at the end of each employer visit to make notes. The good news is if you stay less than the allotted time with any organization, you can add the extra time to your "special twenty minutes" used for returning to the employers you think are worth a second visit.

Move on to your next chosen organization and do just as you had done before. If you discover that you really are not interested in a company, move on – politely but quickly.

Review of your visits

It is now time to take stock of your visits and to select those employers you feel are worthy of another visit to express your genuine interest. If you did not meet the most senior representative on your first visit, try to do so on the second but be subtle. You don't want to insult anyone by implying that meeting them was not sufficient. Tell them that you are very interested and

Plan ahead for career fairs. Prepare your questions and think about what you want to achieve from visiting with companies. Utilize this opportunity to your advantage.

Noni Wright
Recruitment & Selection
Coordinator,
TransAlta Utilities Corporation

ask them a few more questions. You should be far more knowledgeable at this point so this should not be a problem. Do not make a nuisance of yourself but stay long enough to ensure they know who you are and that they will remember you.

After the fair

It is crucial that you take some time, as soon after the fair as possible, to make extensive notes and to organize all the material you have gathered while the information is still fresh in your mind. Now is the time to start building a file on each of the companies you intend to pursue further.

Job Fairs

These differ from Career Fairs in that they are events where organizations that have actual openings come to do their recruiting. They are also referred to as Interview Fairs, Career Exchanges and Interview Clearinghouses. They can include as few as a half dozen employers and or as many as a hundred. If you decide that you want to include attendance at Job Fairs in your campaign, I strongly suggest you read on because they can be very time consuming. Remember, that in most cases the employers attending will be recruiting for their immediate needs.

Job Fairs generally fall into two categories: those that are open to all and those that are industry and/or experience specific.

The good news is that they are usually widely advertised in newspapers and trade magazines and most provide detailed information with respect to which employers will be attending.

Before you head out to one of the fairs, find out if employers will be looking for entry level people. In most cases, job fair organisers are very specific about the technical requirements for the positions that are being recruited. Geographic locations are usually given as well. Where the advertisements for a Job Fair do not stipulate the exact level of experience required, call ahead to find out more. As with Career Fairs, try to get a list of employers attending as early as possible so that you can do your research before attending. Most don't charge for attending.

The toughest part is the first contact with an employer, breaking the ice at a cocktail party or a career day.

Marie-Josée Letendre
Audit Intermediate,
Richter, Usher & Vineberg,
University of Montreal Grad '93

Start early, keep contact. It can be very important, short and long term.

Bruce Walker
Coordinator, Recruitment
Union Gas Ltd.

39

You should be prepared to come armed with your resume and CACEE form as well as your transcript. It is also essential, now more so than ever, that you have an impressive opening with which to address employer representatives you meet.

A good opening line you may want too use is "I've heard a lot about the company and I've been eagerly awaiting the opportunity to meet a recruiter from the organization". They'll probably ask you what you've heard. This will provide you with the ideal opportunity to let them know the high quality research you've done.

Be dressed to be interviewed because it is very likely, if chosen, you will be interviewed right on the spot. Do not expect to get a job right then and there. If the employer is impressed, the process will continue with a follow up interview on the premises.

Cocktail Parties

The early evening cocktail party is a fundamental part of the "real world". Whether it is a charity event or a business function prior to a dinner, the cocktail party is here to stay and is becoming a regular part of the on-campus routine. They can be held following a Career Fair, prior to an awards luncheon or often they are sponsored by a professional association, group or individual club or organization.

Many students find these events particularly difficult because they are so foreign to your everyday lives. The thought of walking up to a stranger, often much older than you, and introducing yourself can be very intimidating.

But the following steps will make a cocktail party situation less frightening and will enable you to obtain maximum benefit from each event.

Dress

Make sure you find out from the organizers what the appropriate dress is. If you are unable to find out, dress in business attire. You can dress down far more easily than you can dress up at the last moment. Even if you are over dressed, you'll feel less conspicuous than if you are the only person in jeans.

First impressions are critical – them of you and you of them.

Jennifer Young
Chair, Department of Co-operative Education, The University College of the Cariboo

This part is the most exciting! You can learn a lot over a casual conversation. People like to talk so all you have to do is ask.

Dawn Ursuliak
Risk Management Analyst, TransAlta Utilities Corporation, University of Alberta Grad '93

You may be disappointed if you fail, but you are doomed if you don't try.

Beverly Sills

Arrival time

Arrive a little earlier than the scheduled time. This will enable you to get accustomed to the surroundings before the majority of the people arrive. It will also mean that you will not have to walk into a crowded room and break into the circles that have formed. It will give you an opportunity to meet recruiters who have arrived early. As the evening unfolds, however, you will find that recruiters are constantly surrounded by students, but early on in the evening they too will be looking for people to talk to.

The party

As soon as you arrive walk around the room once to get a feel for the surroundings.

I recommend you do this until you feel comfortable in the cocktail party setting. I suggest you get a soft drink and then plan to approach your first employer. Always keep your drink in your left hand. Your right hand should always be ready to shake hands. The same "left hand only" rule applies to food. If you feel the need to eat, stick to finger food and only use your left hand. You do not want your right hand to feel greasy or cold when you shake someone's hand.

When introducing yourself to a recruiter step up to the person, shake his or her hand firmly, look them in the eye and say your name clearly. Tell the person a little bit about yourself: "Hello my name is John Wilson, and I am graduating with a degree in finance in April". If you then ask the recruiter to tell you about their company, you've demonstrated that you've not done any research. Instead, ask them questions about what they are looking for in students, their training programs, and the type of work you would do in the first year. These aspects of the job are far more difficult to research and are legitimate questions at this stage of the process.

Be prepared for the small talk that is inevitable at every cocktail party. The weather and sports, the food and drink are typical topics. Even at this early stage you are being judged, so be careful not to be critical or negative.

If you are one of a group of students talking to a recruiter, make sure you participate in the conversation but never try to dominate it. Skilled recruiters will always make a note of two types of behaviour at cocktail parties. People

Be aware of current affairs... i.e. economic trends and current issues affecting the company.

Roger Lemay
Manager, Recruitment Services,
CP Rail System

(Networking) Do it constantly.

Kelly Smith
Regional Manager,
London Life Insurance Co.

You cannot find another venue that offers such a great opportunity to interact with employers with such a limit in the down side risk.

Jim Kelly
Director, Career Planning and
Placement, Queen's University

who are rude and will not let other students participate in the conversation and students who stand idly by in the group and do not participate at all.

It is important to remember that unless you are alone with the recruiter, the questions you ask should be generic, of interest to all in the group, and asked loudly enough so that everyone in the group can hear them.

Once you feel you have stayed long enough to get useful information on the organization and feel assured that you have made a positive impression on the recruiter, it is time to move on. The three best tactics to use to move on are:

Excuse yourself to go to the washroom;
You need to refill your drink, all the talking you are doing is
making you thirsty;
You need to give other people a chance to meet the recruiter.

Make sure you get the recruiter's business card before you leave. This is a great opportunity to mention your name once again, particularly if you are not wearing a name tag. Give him or her one of your cards if you have any.

If you are successfully meeting a number of new people, I strongly suggest you take periodic note breaks during the course of the event. The washroom is the best place to do this. Make sure you record all the important information you have gathered and a brief description of each of the recruiters you have met. The best place is on the back of their business card.

At the end of the evening, transcribe these notes to the files you are starting to compile for each of the organizations.

Breakfasts, Luncheons and Dinners

More and more, student organizations have climbed on the bandwagon and are hosting breakfasts, luncheons and dinners throughout the year and inviting organizations that recruit graduating students to attend. These events are becoming more common as students are seeing the value of attending these events to meet these recruiters.

Your attitude towards these events must be positive. They are hard work but you should take advantage of these excellent networking opportunities.

Unless you have already secured employment, you must view these as ideal opportunities to meet and impress recruiters, and not as social events to mix with your friends.

As is the case with the cocktail parties, arrive early. Many of the events start with a stand-up reception of some type and are ideal opportunities to meet recruiters other than those with whom you will be sitting for the meal. The same advice that I gave you concerning cocktail parties applies to these events. Just remember, the more time you spend at these events, the more contacts you will make and the more your networking ability will improve.

The meal itself is probably one of the most difficult networking activities and is undoubtedly the reason why some students avoid these events. I'll handle this later in the chapter on second interviews.

Organization Information Sessions

If you are interested in an organization, it is essential that you attend their information session. Not only will you learn vital information about the company but it is once again an excellent opportunity to meet recruiters. Many organizations take attendance at these sessions and if you're not present, you can be expected to be asked why if they interview you.

Attendance is crucial because over and above giving you information on the organization, they will often provide you with insight into what qualities they are looking for in the people they want to hire. This knowledge is integral to tailoring the cover letter and resume you will be sending to the organization. Arrive early for the session. If this is impossible try to stay after the formal presentation is over. Introduce yourself as described in the paragraph on cocktail parties. Tell the representative that you are interested in the organization and why. If it's after the session, ask the recruiter a question or two. Remember you would like them to remember you positively, so ask the question clearly. Make sure you are not asking for information that was covered in the session or that would be easily uncovered through basic research.

The firm I was most interested in never received my ACCIS (CACEE) form. Luckily I had attended so many recruiting events that the HR people were expecting my form; when they didn't receive it, they called me. Three weeks later I accepted their offer for summer employment.

Lisa Adelstein
Supervisor,
Richter, Usher & Vineberg,
McGill University Grad '92

Conclusion

The more of these events you attend the more you will become known to the recruiters and the more self confident you will become. Do not take the attitude that if you have met the recruiters once, you do not need to see them again. The more accustomed you are to the type of event and the surroundings, the better you will feel and the more you will radiate poise and maturity. Keep remembering recruiters love to hire people with whom they feel comfortable. The more time they spend with you, the more at ease they will feel.

Try to talk to recruiters. Get their names and/or business cards and mention that you spoke to them at the fair when you write your cover letter.

Zina Principato
Assistant to Operations Engineer,
Union Gas Ltd.
McMaster University Grad '94

Cover Letters

4

Your cover letter will be the first thing most people will read. There are three circumstances that will cause you to write to an organization in the initial stages of the recruiting process:

You are applying directly for a position;
You are trying to open a door to a company that may not be recruiting at that particular time, or for your level of experience;
You are simply trying to persuade a networking contact to meet with you for a half an hour.

The key word is persuasion. Unless you are applying for a position through your on-campus career centre and the employer has said no cover letters are required, the cover letter will always be the first thing read.

What you are trying to ensure is that it is not the only thing read. You have to entice the reader to read on. You must, therefore, provide them with incentive to read the attached resume and ultimately to want to meet you. I will deal with these three scenarios where you will most likely need to send a cover letter.

General advice about cover letters

Think of the letter as a sales pitch. The cover of your autobiography, the commercial for your product – you!

Ideally, it should be one page in length and no more than four paragraphs.

Use high quality paper and don't choose a flashy colour.

Avoid addressing the letter "to whom it may concern" at all costs. Unless you direct it to a specific person, you have no control over who will see your letter and resume and even more importantly, who will not.

Give both the resume and cover letter a focus or don't bother sending them.

Jim Kelly
Director, Career Planning & Placement, Queen's University

Never ever use a standard cover letter with a space where the addressee's name will be entered and then handwrite the name. While the concept may seem far-fetched, about twenty percent of the cover letters I have received over the last year were addressed in this way, even though an addressee's name appeared in the advertisement. This conveys the clear message that you don't really care. Instead, make the reader believe the letter is a personal one.

Make one hundred percent sure that the name of the organization and the addressee are spelled correctly. If you have the slightest doubt, call the organization and ask.

Make sure that it is free of typographical, spelling and grammatical errors.

The letter should indicate your understanding of the job, the company and should state why you are an excellent candidate. It should draw interest and attention to your resume. It should not be a summary of it.

Where the advertisement calls for specific technical skills, make sure that those you possess are clearly and concisely stated in the letter.

Applications for a specific position

Begin the letter by referring to the specific position being advertised. If a position reference number is quoted, use it and put it in bold type. More than one opening may exist and you want to make sure your letter is directed to the right place.

The second paragraph is very important, for it is here that you should state why you are worthy of further consideration, why your resume should not go directly to the reject pile. Tell them what you are looking for and state your qualifications. These should include why you believe you're the right person for the job and what you can contribute to the organization. By including something relevant about the company and tying it to your qualifications, you will certainly send the message to the reader that you are not sending your resume blindly to any position you see advertised.

The third paragraph is your opportunity to highlight your significant achievements and your special qualities, your enticement for the reader to want to meet you.

Target your job search – don't do mass mailings! Remember, thousands of graduates convocate every year – what have you done to differentiate yourself?

Dana Tonus
Director, Co-operative Education
& Student Placement,
University of Windsor

The objective of the fourth paragraph is to request an interview and to make it as easy as possible for the recruiters to reach you. In the past, I have received resumes and chosen the candidates to be interviewed only to be thwarted in my attempts to ever reach the candidate. Some have left me so frustrated that I end up with a negative opinion of them before I ever meet them. Leave phone numbers where you know you can be reached or where you have an answering machine. If you know you are going to be home at specific times, state these times. It will make the recruiter's life that much easier. If you have a fax number or E-mail address, include it.

Answering machines

A word of warning about answering machines and those answering the phone on your behalf. If you usually have an outrageous message on your machine, change it immediately to one that sounds businesslike. Make sure the machine is switched on at all times. For those of you who don't live alone, now is the time to have a meeting with all those who potentially may answer your phone. It is essential that you get their cooperation in ensuring the phone is answered courteously and that proper messages are taken. In addition, you will want to stress the importance of your receiving the messages promptly.

I remember calling a candidate a while ago and being greeted by a younger brother who tried to convince me that I had in fact reached the "city morgue". On another memorable occasion, when calling to invite a candidate to a second interview, I was faced with a mother who insisted on knowing how their child had performed in the first interview and wanting to know what chance I felt they had of getting the job.

When you are not responding to an advertisement

These letters fall into two categories: when you have a contact in the organization and when you don't.

In the first scenario, it is essential that you address your letter to the person who will be able to take appropriate action. You must, in your opening sentence, mention the name of your contact person and what your relationship is to this person. Most of the basic suggestions for cover letters still apply.

If you have an answering machine, make sure the taped message is professional.

Noreen Teo
Internal Auditor, Union Gas Ltd.,
McMaster University Grad '94

When you don't have a contact person, call the company to ask to whom employment inquiries should be addressed. Do not be put off if the person to whom you are speaking tells you there are no openings. They simply may not know.

In both cases, the most important thing to remember is that you make your letter specific as to the type of position for which you are applying. All too often, recruiters receive unsolicited letters stating that the writer is interested in "a position" with the organization. Any position? Are you leaving the choice of position up to the recruiter? Are you asking the recruiter to read your cover letter and resume and decide what kind of a person you are, what your long and short term goals are and then decide for which of the fifty positions in the organization you would best be suited? This type of letter implies that the onus of career direction is left to someone who has never met you.

A "door-opening" cover letter

You will also often be writing to persuade a networking contact to meet with you for a half an hour.

The letter again should be short and to the point. It is important that you introduce yourself in the opening paragraph and explain your connection to the person to whom you are writing.

The second paragraph should explain the purpose for your meeting and the expected length of the meeting. Your appreciation for the time given should be real but not overly flowery. Unlike in an application for a position, you should state in the final paragraph that you will be calling the addressee to arrange a meeting for a specific day and time. If the day and time are inconvenient, it is likely they will call you to set up the meeting at another time.

OLIVIA J. ABBOTT
4516 Darby Way
Halifax, Nova Scotia
B4X 1C7

January 19, 1996.

Mr. John R. Martin
Director, Human Resources
Saskatoon Computers Inc.
465 Marilyn Drive
Saskatoon, Saskatchewan
S7Y 8J9

Dear Mr. Martin:

I was recently speaking with my uncle, James Jackson, about opportunities in the computer programming industry and he recommended that I contact you. I will be graduating this Spring from the Technical University of Nova Scotia with a Bachelor's degree in Computer Science and I am interested in working for your company as a Computer Programmer.

As you will see from my resume I have a well-rounded background, through my university education and practical experience. I have gained invaluable experience in my work as a Research Associate. I am extremely proud of my involvement in many extracurricular activities. In 1992, I received a prestigious award for my volunteer work in the community.

I am confident that my courses at the Technical University of Nova Scotia in software engineering and applications programming, coupled with my work experience, will prove particularly useful for the position of Computer Programmer at Saskatoon Computers Inc. Although I am presently living in Nova Scotia, I am willing to relocate in order to pursue my career.

I have included my resume for your consideration. I can be reached at (902) 555-6715 after 3pm. and on weekends or by E-mail at O_Abbott@hauk.sas.ca.

Sincerely,

Olivia J. Abbott

enc.

Dora Smith
2802 Davis Rd.
Toronto, Ontario
M8C 5M7
(416) 555-6502

January 16, 1996.

Wright, Auger & Harrow
1256 Market Ave.
Toronto, Ontario
M4L 2P3

Attn: Janice Peck, Human Resources

Dear Ms. Peck:

Are you looking for a competent, motivated, outgoing and well-organized Audit Trainee?

I will be graduating from the University of Toronto in the Spring when I will receive a Bachelor of Commerce in Accounting. I am proud to tell you that I have been on the Dean's List every semester, since I started at university.

As you will see in my resume I have excellent experience in all phases of the accounting profession. In the summer of 1994, I was a summer student at Robbins & Richard where I worked directly with clients on audits, used a software program called ACCPAC and became familiar with the daily operations of a large accounting firm. In the summer of 1992 and 1993, I was a bookkeeper for an investment company. Since late 1993, I have worked, part time, as an assistant manager for a jewellery store where I am responsible for inventory, bank deposits and balancing the cash. These positions have given me the opportunity to substantially develop my interpersonal skills which will prove invaluable at Wright, Auger and Harrow.

I would like the chance to interview with you at your earliest convenience. It is easiest to reached me at (416) 555-6502 during business hours. Thank you for your consideration.

Sincerely,

Dora Smith

Dora Smith

enc.

DEREK THOMAS
1658 Beacon St. #3A
Winnipeg, Manitoba
R2M 8T3
(204) 555-1921

March 3, 1996.

Mr. George Jacobs
Director of Human Resources
Communications Canada Inc.
1300 River St. W.
Winnipeg, Manitoba
R7B 4H2

Dear Mr. Jacobs:

I am sending you my resume in response to the advertisement you placed in last week's edition of The Winnipeg Free Press for the position of an entry level public relations trainee **(reference number FR391)**.

I will be graduating this Spring from the University of Manitoba with a Bachelor's Degree in Labour Studies. My experience as captain of the school's intercollegiate hockey team has taught me outstanding communication and interpersonal skills. It has also given me an opportunity to deal extensively with the media. Throughout my years at school, in addition to my involvement in sports, I have held a part time position at a retail store. As proof of my discipline and organizational abilities, I have been able to work thirty hours each week and still maintain good grades.

I am interested in beginning my career in the communications industry, in the field of public relations and I feel my experience, energy and enthusiasm would enable me to make an excellent contribution at Communications Canada Inc.

I can be reached at the above address and telephone number, or a message can be left at (204) 287-3865.

Sincerely,

Derek Thomas

enc.

PIERRE FAUCHER
26 Haley Rd.
Montreal, Quebec
H9H 9P3
(514) 555-9046

November 17, 1995.

Mr. Andre Cartier
Director, Human Resources
Farallon, Inc.
787 E. Fourier Drive
Montreal, Quebec
H6T 7Y2

Dear Mr. Cartier:

We met at the Career Fair at McGill University in October last year and at the time you mentioned that your company would be recruiting Junior Systems Analysts this fall, to begin working in September 1996. I am writing to request an interview for one of these positions.

I was impressed by how helpful the staff from your organization was at the Career Fair. Your plans to create a department dealing solely with New Applications Development is of particular interest to me, given my background.

I will be graduating from McGill University in June with a Bachelor of Commerce in Management Information Systems. I received the James McGill Scholarship in 1994 for my excellent grades. My course work has included programming, database management and systems analysis. In addition, I have been the assistant to a PhD student who is creating a new business software program for his thesis. I am confident these skills will give me the ideal background required for the position of junior systems analyst at Farallon Inc.

I will contact you early in December to set up an interview at your earliest convenience. Thank you for your consideration.

Sincerely,

Pierre Faucher

Pierre Faucher

enc.

Cover letter checklist

Is your cover letter one page and no more than four paragraphs?

Did you use high quality stationery that is 8 1/2 by 11 inches?

Is your cover letter addressed to a specific person and not merely "to whom it may concern"?

Is the name of the organization and addressee's name spelled correctly?

Is your letter free of spelling errors and typos?

Is it visually appealing?

Does your cover letter demonstrate your understanding of the position for which you are applying?

In the first paragraph, did you state which position you are applying for and the reference number (if applicable)?

Did you state, in the second paragraph, why you are worthy of further consideration? (eg. your qualifications)

Did you highlight your major, significant achievements and special qualities in the third paragraph?

In the fourth paragraph, did you ask for an interview and give your phone and fax numbers and E-mail address (if you have one) or state when you would be contacting the organization?

At the end of the letter, did you express your gratitude to the addressee for taking the time to consider your application?

Did you sign the letter?

Did you remember to enclose a copy of your resume?

Is the envelope visually pleasing?

Does the name and address of the addressee appear correctly and professionally on the envelope?

What would I have to do to get you to notice me too? Do I stand in line – one of a million admiring eyes? Walk the tightrope way up high, write your name across the sky?

Donna Summers

Resumes

5

Why You Need One

There is probably more written on the preparation of your resume than on any other single aspect of job search. Whether you are looking for a summer internship, a graduating position, a job overseas or you're already earning more than $100,000, there is a specific guide to help you prepare your resume.

Does a graduating student need one? Do you need a resume even if you don't have years of experience? The answer is emphatically yes. Unless you are going to work in the family business, you will need a resume to get an interview and ultimately, a job. The common misconception is that only people with work experience need a resume. You may not have a lot of work experience but as you will soon discover, work is certainly not all that will appear in your resume. In fact, it will only account for about forty percent at this time of your life.

There are those who would still support getting rid of the resume completely and relying entirely on one's network to secure a job. My belief is that even if you have a great network and are able to secure an "in" at your most desired target organization, they will still want to see your resume before they see you.

A resume is best described as the sales material to sell a product to a potential customer. You. To a possible employer. Remember that throughout the marketing process your objective is to sell your product (you) to the market (that group of employers looking to acquire someone with your skills and background).

Graduating students' resumes will generally use one of two formats. The standard free-form resume that is covered in most job search literature

Where I was born and where and how I have lived is unimportant. It is what I have done with where I have been that should be of interest.

Georgia O'Keeffe

55

and the fixed format resume, the CACEE (ACCIS) form, used by many on-campus recruiters.

Most of the suggestions I'll make throughout this chapter will apply equally to both types. I will begin with general advice on the preparation of resumes, then deal more specifically with CACEE forms. Throughout the general section I will refer to resumes even though, in recruiting parlance, the other format is called an ACCIS form.

General Rules and Guidelines

1. Ensure there are no gaps of time in your resume. A gap may cause the reader to assume that you have something to hide. Once you've decided on the time-frame your resume is going to cover, you must account for the entire period.

2. Each resume should be tailored to the employer's needs as much as possible. Before the advent of personal computers, the preparation of a tailored resume was extremely time consuming and costly. As a result, most people opted for a generic resume. Resumes tailored to the specific requirements of a position have now become essential. You should address the employer's needs and interests as specifically as you can in each one you send out. The objective is to emphasize your strengths and how you might fit within the organization, while playing down your weaknesses as the specific job requirements dictate.

3. The proper preparation of a resume takes time. Those prepared in a hurry are easily detected by experienced recruiters. While it is not always the case, you have to believe that your resume is being evaluated by a very experienced employer. Hopefully, this will ensure that you strive for excellence, knowing that anything less will probably result in elimination.

Students we polled say they take upwards of six hours to prepare their resume, not including computer time. My suggestion is that you prepare it over a period of a week or more, rather than in one sitting. Start by brainstorming ideas and continue this throughout the process. Each time you return to the process you will be pleasantly surprised at how much more you remember about things you have done. In addition, each review seems to

Put a lot of thought into your resume. Try to differentiate yourself. Show the employer why you will benefit them.

Lorie Gibson
Accountant/Analyst,
DuPont Canada Inc.,
Wilfrid Laurier University Grad '94

reveal errors that you previously overlooked, plus it improves the wording and the format.

4. Keep in mind throughout the preparation that, along with your cover letter (if one is sent), your resume is a stand-alone document. You will not be present when the recruiters screen it for further explanations or for clarification of any ambiguities.

5. Use reverse chronological order to list your education, work experience and awards. In other words, start with your most recent accomplishments and work backwards.

6. Remember that when you are faxing your resume to a potential employer you cannot control the quality of the fax received. Always follow up by sending an original.

7. How long should a resume be? Some recently published job search guides say that for a graduating student, it should never be more than one page. A student I recently spoke to had used one of these guides to prepare her resume. She was applying for a job as a Trainee Systems Analyst in a company specialising in the retail industry. She was not initially selected for an interview primarily because, unlike many of her "competitors", she did not appear to have any retail experience. I explained this when she called me to ask why she hadn't been selected for an interview. It was then that she told me that she had, in fact, worked as a retail sales person two summers but she hadn't included it because she didn't have room on her one page resume. She was under the mistaken impression that restricting her resume to one page was more important than including relevant experience. Your resume should be long enough to include all relevant experience and never be shortened if it means omitting a crucial piece of experience that could be key to being chosen for the interview. For graduating students this need not be longer than two pages.

8. Always keep in mind the importance of making the resume easy to read and concise. If the advertisement asks for specific technical job requirements, ensure they "stand out" in the resume.

9. Ultimately you will have to supply references to employers. I do not believe it is necessary to include these on your resume. The ACCIS (CACEE) form does not provide space for references. You should have this

Nothing in the world can take the place of persistence. Talent will not; nothing is more common than unsuccessful men with talent. Genius will not; unrewarded genius is almost a proverb. Education will not; the world is full of educated derelicts. Persistence and determination alone are omnipotent!

Calvin Coolidge

The toughest part of getting a job was the waiting and the wondering.

Dawn Ursuliak
Risk Management Analyst,
TransAlta Utilities Corporation,
University of Alberta Grad '93

57

list prepared in advance, however, ready to be handed out at any stage in the process. Once again, these should be tailored to each position for which you are applying.

Be prepared! This means knowing what the job is and matching your skills and abilities to the requirements.

Cindy Stephenson
Director, Faculty of Management,
University of Manitoba

10. The objective is for your resume to stand out in the crowd. This should be because of the contents and not because it really does "stand out". Unless specifically asked for in the advertisement, you should avoid any of the following popular attempts to make yours stand out:

   Using coloured paper Remember that in many cases, the person doing the screening is doing so from a photocopy rather than the original. Think of how poorly red, green or pink paper photocopies before you go ahead and prepare your resume on a colour other than white, cream or gray.

   Binding your resume Again, remember that the resumes are often photo-copied. If you go ahead and bind it, hope it doesn't get ruined when photocopied.

   Enclosing a photograph Unless they are specifically requested, do not enclose a photograph of yourself.

   Using a variety of type fonts, sizes and graphic styles Unless this is the field you are in and you are trying to show your expertise, this should not be done. It makes for very difficult reading.

11. After you have completed the first draft of your resume, have someone who knows you well review it. More than likely, they will immediately think of things you have forgotten. Continue this review process throughout your resume preparation. He or she can certainly, objectively, tell you if the resume sends out a clear and accurate picture of you. Ask them to check for spelling errors and typos. An extra pair of eyes is helpful in spotting that extra little mistake.

12. Use your full name as it appears on your official school transcripts. If you are commonly called by another name, it should appear (in brackets) following your name.

13. Many large organizations are looking into computerized scanning of resumes. Be sure you keep current on their requirements and what you will have to do to meet their needs as scanning becomes more commonplace.

14. Include both the address where you are currently living and your permanent home address if you are living away from home. You should include phone numbers at both addresses and, if you have them, fax numbers and E-mail contact as well. Your name should appear on each page of your resume.

15. Do not include comments about your health, weight or give your social insurance number unless they are specifically requested. There is no need to state your marital status, religion or political affiliation.

16. Avoid obvious fillers that appear to only take up space and do little to add to a reader's knowledge of you. Most of these seem to appear in the Personal Interest section of a resume. Examples include:

Love listening to music   Getting together with friends
Travel   Aerobics
People person   Dining out
Reading

The Screening Process

The screening of resumes is the toughest part of the process for the recruiting organization. It is a time consuming process and often becomes an all consuming task for recruiters when faced with hundreds or thousands of resumes. Many recruiters cannot devote sufficient time to this part of the process. They often end up screening the resumes between other major tasks, while talking on the phone, during their commute to work or in front of their television set at home. Don't think that a panel of recruiters sits in a room and spends a half an hour reviewing each resume deciding which people to interview. They are forced to make quick decisions, under difficult circumstances, often with too little information about you.

Make yourself necessary to somebody.

Ralph Waldo Emerson

The 'NO' pile

When screening entry level resumes, recruiters are usually faced with hundreds more resumes than interview spaces and many more interview slots than available positions. Therefore, to begin the screening process, they will initially be looking for reasons to eliminate candidates and add to their "NO" pile. The more resumes they can eliminate in this way, the easier and the faster their review process will be. Remember, to make their pile of resumes more manageable, they will almost immediately discard every resume with spelling errors, typos and poor presentation. Throughout the screening process they will be looking for reasons to reject your resume.

The 'YES' pile

Resume reviewers are constantly searching through the piles of applications for the resumes of candidates that they believe will be the future "stars" in their organizations. Each time they find one of those "can't miss" candidates they think will be a fast tracker in the organization, they automatically put that resume into the "Yes" pile. The obvious question is how do you get your resume into that pile. Obviously, each organization and each individual recruiter has his or her own criteria.

If you have met the organization's representatives previously and they were impressed with you, they will be on the lookout for your resume. They will then look for reasons to include you in their "Yes" Pile. Many recruiters will immediately divide the resumes into two piles, one for those candidates they have met and one for those they have not. More often than not, more candidates will be selected for interviews from the pile of candidates they know than from those they don't.

From those in the "we know" pile, they are looking for confirmation of their initial assessment. Once they find it, they will often include you in their list of candidates to be interviewed. For those they haven't met, the only way you can avoid the intense scrutiny and the numbers game that will follow as they try to pare down their numbers, is either to have accomplished something exceptional, unusual or interesting, or have outstanding work related experience.

Examples of events in your past that will excite recruiters:

1. You are in the first one or two percent in your class.
2. You have won academic scholarships, awards, bursaries or other similar prizes.
3. You have been responsible for starting a club, charity organization, sports league or team.

I am easily satisfied with the very best.

Winston Churchill

Oh, the things you can think up if only you try!

Dr. Seuss

4. You are, or have been, president, chairperson or captain of a club, charity organization, sports league or team.

5. You have coached a sports team of any kind, at any level and for any age players.

6. You have teaching, tutoring, instructing or marking experience.

7. You have worked in a foreign country.

8. You have travelled alone or to exotic places.

9. You have worked for a "glamour" employer. Professional sports teams, Disney and the United Nations are examples.

10. You have received Community Awards of Distinction.

11. You have a pilot's licence, SCUBA certificates or parachuting experience.

12. You have received a Black Belt in any Martial Art form.

13. You have held unusual or obscure jobs. A character at Canada's Wonderland, an actor at an historic site or a tourist attraction, working as a page for the Parliament in Ottawa, or a fishing guide in a remote resort are examples I have seen recently. Even tree-planting, while far more common these days, still attracts curiosity and interest, and indicates that you are not just tenacious, but adaptable and are able to meet goals.

Look long and hard into your past to try and find something special that you have done. It need not be one of the suggestions above, but rather something that will allow you to stand out in the crowd.

Having any one of these accomplishments on your resume will not necessarily guarantee you an interview but a combination of any of these and a well prepared resume will go a long way to getting you onto the interview list.

When completing CACEE forms which are being used in conjunction with resumes, make certain that the CACEE form is fully completed. Do not leave sections incomplete with the notation "see attached resume" as this will convey a message of laziness to the potential employer.

Ernie Hovell
Director, Career Planning &
Employment Centre,
Acadia University

Format

There are many different formats for resumes. The most common of these are chronological, functional and combination.

Chronological

A chronological resume is done in reverse date order and highlights a strong, steady work and schooling history. It is the most common format for students.

Advantages

It provides employers with a clear and concise assessment of your life and experience.

It highlights most students' major asset, their education.

If you have had a lot of work experience, it will be highlighted.

Drawbacks

If you do not have steady or relevant work experience, it is definitely emphasized.

It exposes gaps in work experience.

It does not allow you to build on the transferability of various skills from one job to another.

Functional

This is done in a format listing skills, abilities and accomplishments rather than work experience.

Advantages

You can draw from all aspects of your experience skills relevant to the position. This means that paid jobs and volunteer positions will be emphasised equally.

If you have not had steady work experience, this fact will not be highlighted. This type of resume is particularly useful if you are re-entering the workforce, or if much of your work history consists of part time, freelance or contract work.

You can include work you have done and experience you have gained on projects, term papers and research as part of your experience and skills.

Drawbacks

It does not show the amount of work experience you have gained.

Some recruiters may think you are trying to hide something in your past, such as previous employer's names or work experiences of particularly short duration.

Some recruiters may find this style more difficult to follow and to compare candidates.

Combination

This, as it states, is a combination of the two formats. Usually it starts by stating a career objective followed by accomplishments and capabilities, education and then a summarized work history.

Advantages

It has all the advantages of both previously described formats.

The reader is immediately faced with your best qualities and you can really tailor each resume to each job's specifications.

It can be particularly useful if your relevant experience is scattered across a number of areas in your resume. This is accomplished by pulling all the relevant experience together in the "accomplishments and capabilities" section.

Drawbacks

They tend to be longer and require far more preparation time and effort in designing, formating and writing than the other styles discussed.

Can be confusing unless the presentation is clear and concise.

Structure

Irrespective of the format you choose, the following common elements must be present in all resumes:

Your name, address and contact numbers (phone, fax, E-mail)
Education history
Special skills, abilities and accomplishments
Work experience
Extracurricular activities and interests

Education history

Many students feel that this is the easiest section because they only have to state the facts. I believe, even in this primarily factual part of the resume, there is a need to sell your academic qualifications as well.

Ensure that your dates are correct and always indicate clearly when you are graduating. If you plan to start work other than immediately upon graduation, you should state that fact as well.

The name of the university or college you are attending and the specific degree or diploma you have received, or are going to receive, are statements of fact, but there are other aspects you will want to highlight. You may want to state all the courses you have taken, research papers you have written, or presentations you have made that are relevant to the position for which you are applying. You should also include program and course descriptions where they highlight skills that are pertinent for the position.

Students often ask me if they should add their grade point average or overall marks at the end of the section. Many organizations will ask you to include your transcript with your application. If it is not requested, you should definitely include your grades if you think it is going to strengthen your application. If you know how you rank in your class and you rank in the top twenty-five percent, include this in your resume along with your GPA. If you do not have an official ranking system, you are going to have to judge for yourself how you rank and act accordingly. If your marks in your degree major or in courses that are relevant to the particular job for which you are applying are impressive, you certainly should include those.

Dave Uez, Manager, Human Resources Development, AT&T Global Information Systems, had the following comment on the question of marks: "Grades are important because it shows you want to achieve results. Don't tell us you are just there to learn and grades aren't important to you".

Despite frequent comments like these from recruiters, many students feel that recruiters place too much emphasis on grades. Regardless of how you may feel about a recruiter's emphasis on marks, they are a fact of life. Remember that in most cases, marks are the only tangible criteria a recruiter has to use.

Does this mean that you will never get a job if your grades are not good? The following two comments from two very experienced Career Educators will put this into perspective and provide you with sound advice.

Floyd Visser, Supervisor, Program and Employment Resource Centre, Southern Alberta Institute of Technology, notes "Recognize that grades are important but not all important". This view was shared and further illustrated by Jan Basso, Director of Career Services, Wilfrid Laurier University, who said "We frequently hear employers say that they are more than willing

Emphasize technical skills acquired outside of your courses. If you don't have much, emphasize skills you obtained in the courses rather than just naming them.

Debbie Ng
Software Designer,
Unisys GSG Canada Inc.,
McGill University Grad '94

to see candidates who don't have an A average but you have to be able to explain why you don't".

The fact that you had a part time job or perhaps you held a time consuming extracurricular position, or that you were ill during a semester or that you initially had difficulty coping with a switch in languages would certainly hold water. Whatever the case, if your marks are below expectations, and there is a legitimate reason, ensure you clearly and unemotionally explain it in your cover letter or resume. Do not wait to explain it "in person" at the interview. You may not get one and then you will never have the opportunity to explain your reasons. If you have met the recruiters doing the screening and they have been impressed with you, they will be far more tolerant of grades that don't quite meet their expectations.

A student a few years ago had a grade point average that was well below the average. Believing that recruiters might not look beyond the first page of her ACCIS form, she put a note where her marks should have appeared referring to an explanation on the last page of her form.

I did not go directly to this page, but reviewed the rest of the form. I was very impressed with her explanation on the last page.

"I have a 2.60 GPA. I know my marks are below your expectations but I would like to inform you that I have played on the intercollegiate basketball team and worked twenty hours a week at two part time jobs since I started university". This drew a positive response from a number of recruiting firms. We were successful in hiring her and once she was able to concentrate on one thing, as expected, she excelled.

Skills, achievements and extracurricular activities

The format you choose for your resume will dictate whether your personal experiences and achievements should be covered in one section or done separately. On the CACEE form, each is a separate section. For ease of explanation, I will treat them as one category.

This is the section of your resume which allows you the most freedom in emphasizing your skills and accomplishments from all aspects of life. It is your opportunity to evaluate everything you've done and extract what is relevant for the skills needed for the position to which you are applying. Unlike the work experience or education section of your resume where

This is your marketing tool, so ensure you highlight how you would contribute to the organization, what benefits you offer, and your interest in the employer and position.

Ann-Marie Elliott
Placement Services Coordinator,
York University

65

you're restricted by dates, time and specific facts that must be shown, here you're free to include (and exclude!) whatever you choose.

Keep in mind what recruiters are looking for and remember that their ideal person is well-rounded.

Leadership skills and experience

Think carefully about each of the following forms of involvement you may have had. You will benefit by discussing these with friends who may have been involved with you in these activities. The discussion serves to jog your memory and help you to remember the wonderful things you may have accomplished in your past.

High School, College, CEGEP and University

yearbook	clubs
fund raising	sports teams
honour roll	sports awards
valedictorian	event coordinator
school plays	tutoring
school band	school newspaper
student council	graduation dance or ceremony
academic awards, prizes and scholarships	counsellor

Community

volunteer work	coordinating fund raising events
directing meetings	visits to the elderly
organizing parties or festivals	baseball, tennis, swimming coach
Sunday School teacher	

Licences, Accreditations and Training Certificates

St John's Ambulance	Royal Lifesaving Society of Canada
CPR Certificate	martial arts accreditation

Target your resume to the company and position you are applying for. Emphasize leadership and communication skills, since these are more important than simply a high GPA.

Patrick Farajian
Network Designer,
Bell-Northern Research,
McGill University Grad '94

Work experience

Ideally, an organization looks for a candidate with work experience in a directly related field. This is a rare find, however, so the fact that you have worked at all will always be regarded as positive. This applies to both the summer positions and part time work during school. The old adage that any work is better than no work at all holds true.

Unfortunately, there is little that can be done about the work experience you have had to this point. A part time job, even this semester, would certainly add some weight to your resume. Describe the positions you have held. Don't insult the readers by telling them what a sales person in a department store or a receptionist in an office does. Only explain special aspects of positions you've held which may not be obvious.

An example of what I mean by "too much" detail is:

Position: Pizza Delivery Person
Responsibilities: Taking orders
Cooking the pizza
Adding up the bill
Delivering the goods
Collecting the money

Showing responsibility

Resume reviewers are particularly impressed by positions that show you have had responsibility and acquired new skills. Highlight these points in each. A steady increase in the level of your responsibility is always impressive. If you've gone from being a busboy to a waiter or waitress in a restaurant or from camper to counsellor-in-training to counsellor, highlight it. Both of these will demonstrate that your supervisors saw enough increased levels of maturity and responsibility to warrant increasing your levels of responsibility – a very impressive progression.

This section gives you the chance to sell both your related and your transferable skills.

State the name of the organizations where you worked, the jobs you held and the dates you worked. Each job should be followed by a very brief description, longer if the position is unusual. At least one significant accom-

Experience is not what happens to a man. It is what a man does with what happens to him.

Aldous Huxley

plishment and relevant new skill you acquired should be included. Try to highlight your ambition and motivation, your work ethic, your organizational skills and your manageability. For example:

Named employee of the month.

Promoted to crew chief.

Became team shift leader after nine months of work. This level is normally only attained after employees have worked for twelve to fifteen months.

Balanced the cash of up to $12,000 and closed the store at the end of the day.

During the past 12 months I have trained eight new employees.

Became the first part-time aerobics instructor to be voted "Best Instructor" by members and staff.

Selected to attend an in-house training program on new design software. This course is normally only offered to full-time employees.

Sold at least 15% over the daily quota, 90% of the time.

Received an "Excellent" rating on an end of a co-op work-term formal performance evaluation.

As a counsellor-in-training, selected to take ten children on an overnight camping trip. Normally, only senior counsellors are given this responsibility.

When you have worked for the same employer for a number of years, ensure that the dates you worked and your responsibilities are clearly indicated. If you worked as a volunteer and you learned a relevant, transferable skill, it may be best to include the description in this section. For example:

Volunteered to co-ordinate a bowl-a-thon to raise money for the Children In Need Foundation, where I learned to perfect my organizational skills. Volunteered to answer phones at a Crisis Centre for Battered Women where I learned to deal calmly and effectively with people in a crisis situation. Recipient of the Outstanding Contribution to Community Life Award for my involvement in volunteer work within my community.

If you held a position of leadership, you may want to mention those job related skills in the section under extracurricular activities.

The Good, the Bad and the Ugly

Over the past year, while preparing this book, I updated a long list of misspelled words, and strange and bizarre phrases I've come across in the resumes and cover letters I've received.

Look carefully at your resume and cover letter and make sure "the bad" ones aren't on yours.

The Bad	The Good
Liason or laison or leaison	Liaison (undoubtedly the most frequently misspelled word)
Laberal or Leberal Arts	Liberal Arts
I am looking for compensation of at least $28,000	I am seeking a salary of at least $28,000
Excellant and excelent	Excellent. Misspelling this word has to cast doubt about your excellence.
The following are my relevant qualities for you to overlook	"Review" or "look over"
Evans High School : 1888-1992	Surely it couldn't have taken that long!
I was in the Honour Roll at my High School	I was on the Honour Roll.
Truely and even, Truelly	Truly
Convienience and convinience	convenience
You will find that I am imminently qualified	eminently
Reciepts and recieved	Receipts and received
Succesful, sucessful and successfull	Successful

Resumes and CACEE application forms are used more to screen people out than screen them in. Therefore take whatever steps necessary to highlight your accomplishments, whether personal or work related, as well as your key personal qualifications and skills that are relevant.

Jill Curley
Career Placement Counsellor,
Student Affairs,
Mount Saint Vincent University

My university has always provided me with a plithora of clubs in which to get involved

If you are going to try and impress people by using uncommon words, at least spell them correctly! (Plethora)

Bookeeping and bookeepping

Bookkeeping

Extracuricular and Extracurriccular

Even though it is preprinted on the CACEE form, this word is regularly misspelled. It is "Extracurricular".

Giutar, violen and paino

Guitar, violin and piano

Ocassionally and occasionaly

Occasionally

Developped or develloped

Developed

Schedualing or schedulling

Scheduling

"Both in the school and work environment, I have learned to deal with computer literacy"

I am still not sure what the applicant was trying to say.

I was responsable for issueing official reciepts.

At least the word "official" was spelled correctly.

Through my education I have exposed myself to

"Been exposed to" or "had exposure to" but never expose yourself, please.

Don't make any errors. Have five people read each draft.

Scott Gregory
Manager of Career Services,
Faculty of Administration,
University of Ottawa

70

Here is a last minute resume checklist of details that definitely make a difference to recruiters.

Did you use good quality paper no larger than 8 1/2" by 11"?

Is your name, address and telephone number (fax and E-mail, if applicable) clearly shown at the top of the first page?

Does your name appear on every page?

Are the dates shown for the schools you attended correct?

Have you clearly indicated your level of proficiency for each of the languages you speak and write?

Have you clearly indicated your level of proficiency for the computer software programs for which you have indicated experience and understanding?

Have you emphasized duties that show your specific skills and accomplishments and avoided those that don't?

Have you shown what you accomplished and what you learned in each job you held?

Have you eliminated all erroneous information that does not directly apply to the position for which you are applying?

Is your resume interesting to read?

Is it visually pleasing?

Have you excluded all "unnecessary" information such as social insurance number, height, weight and marital status?

Did you use action verbs to describe your duties, accomplishments and involvement?

Have you checked all spelling and grammar? Twice? Three times?

Has a third party reviewed your resume to ensure that there are absolutely no spelling or grammar errors?

Did you eliminate activities and involvement that may prejudice the reader, like political affiliations, ethnic background or religious beliefs?

If you have photocopied the form, have the photocopies come out clearly and cleanly?

If you have included a transcript of your courses and marks, has this been clearly and cleanly photocopied?

OLIVIA J. ABBOTT
4516 Darby Way
Halifax, Nova Scotia
B4X 1C7
(902) 555-6715

EDUCATION

1992-1996
Technical University of Nova Scotia
Bachelor of Computer Science
Average 75%

1987-1992
St. Patrick's High School
High School Certificate
Overall Average 72%

HONOURS

May 1992
Rosetti Bursary for Community Involvement. This award was given in recognition of my work with the elderly in the community.

EMPLOYMENT

January to June
1994 (part time)
Technical University of Nova Scotia
Research Associate
Participated in a Scientific Supercomputing Workshop at the University of British Columbia and then co-directed all research concerning supercomputers at TUNS.

January 1994 to
present (part time)
Technical University of Nova Scotia
Teaching Assistant
Responsible for grading all midterms, assignments, research projects and final examinations for the course entitled Introduction to Object-Oriented Programming.

Summer 1994
(full time)
Jack and Jill
Sales Representative
Served customers, replenished stock and created displays. Was given the responsibility of closing the store at the end of the day and acted as assistant manager on week-ends when the full time manager was not present.

Summer 1993
(full time)
Gallop Stables
Stable Hand
Responsible for feeding, training and grooming 15 horses. Developed a new system which decreased the overall time for the procedure by 20 minutes.

EXTRACURRICULAR ACTIVITIES

1988 to present   Volunteer at the Community Centre for the elderly one day a week
1993 to present   Actively involved in fund raising for the Technical University of Nova Scotia

COMPUTER SKILLS

languages: Fortran, Pascal and Basic
software: dBASE, Excel, Corel Draw and AutoCAD software

DORA SMITH
2802 Davis Rd.
Toronto, Ontario
M8C 5M7
(416) 555-6502

EDUCATION

1992-1996	**University of Toronto** Bachelor of Commerce Major: Accounting Minor: Marketing Grade Point Average 3.7/4.3
1988-1992	**Lawrence Park Collegiate** High School Certificate Graduating Average 88% Graduated with Honours

HONOURS

Dean's List (1993, 1994, 1995)
Received a full scholarship for the 1994/1995 academic year

EMPLOYMENT

Summer 1994 (full time)	**Robbins & Richard** *Summer Student* Performed audits and inventory counts. Learned and used ACCPAC, FAST and Excel. Received a 10/10 end of summer evaluation, the highest ever given to a summer student.
November 1993 to present (part time)	**Grant Jewellers** *Assistant Manager* Designed a new system to automatically update inventory records from invoices, prepared daily bank deposits and balanced the cash on a daily basis. Developed a new strategy for displaying merchandise, whereby annual sales increased by 12.5%. Promoted from salesperson to my present position after twelve months.
Summer 1993 and 1992 (full time)	**Investment Strategies Inc.** *Bookkeeper* Prepared and recorded journal entries, reconciled bank statements and assisted the auditor with the preparation of working papers for the fiscal year end.
Summer 1991 (full time)	**Summer Sun Camp** *Senior Camp Counsellor* For eight weeks, I was fully responsible for ten, twelve-year old girls. Taught and evaluated new staff on camp policies and procedures. Promoted from junior counsellor.

EXTRACURRICULAR ACTIVITIES

1990-1991	Editor of high school year book
1995	Journalist for "The Varsity" newspaper
1992-1995	Member of the Accounting Club
1992	Campaign Manager in the student council elections

DEREK THOMAS
1658 Beacon St. #3A
Winnipeg, Manitoba
R2M 8T3
(204) 555-1921
FAX (204) 555-1616

EDUCATION

1992-1996	**University of Manitoba** Bachelor of Arts in Labour Studies Major GPA 3.1/4.5
1989-1992	**John Taylor Collegiate** High School Graduate Certificate Average 78%

EMPLOYMENT

June 1994 to present (part time)	**Dr. Jacob Small** *Receptionist* Developed a new database system using dBASE which saved the doctor and hygienists a considerable amount of time retrieving patient records.
September 1993 to April 1994 (part time)	**Shoe Bazaar** *Shift Manager* Responsible for opening and closing the store. Supervised and trained new employees. Promoted from stock person to salesperson after just three months. Promoted from salesperson to shift manager after one year.
Summer 1993 (full time)	**Fredericton Community Pool** *Lifeguard* Worked as a lifeguard where I planned activities for children, organized a first-aid course for pool members and conducted tests on chlorine levels of the pool each day.

EXTRACURRICULAR ACTIVITIES

1991-present	Active member of the intercollegiate swimming team
1994-present	Involved in fund raising for the swimming team
1992-present	Captain of the Manitoba Bisons (Intercollegiate Hockey Team)
Summer 1992	Backpacked with two friends through Europe for ten weeks where we visited twelve countries.
1991	Volunteered to teach mentally challenged children to ice skate

SPECIAL SKILLS

Hands-on experience using WordPerfect 6.1, dBASE and Lotus 1-2-3 software programs
Fluently bilingual (French and English)
Red Cross Nationals Certificate

PIERRE FAUCHER
26 Haley Road
Montreal, Quebec
H9H 9P3
(514) 555-9046
E-mail: PFaucher@musicb.mcgill.ca

EDUCATION

1993-1996
McGill University
Bachelor of Commerce
Concentrations: Management Information Systems and Entrepreneurship
Grade Point Average 3.8/4

1991-1993
Dawson College
DEC in Commerce Studies
Overall Average 86%

1987-1991
Westmount High School
High School Leaving Certificate
Overall Average 91%

HONOURS

Graduated Westmount High School with honours and a bilingual certificate
Graduated Dawson College with honours
Recipient of the James McGill scholarship in 1994
Placed on the Dean's Honour List each semester at McGill University

EMPLOYMENT

Summer 1995
(full time)
GSR Consulting
Summer Student
Assisted in the development of a user manual for the company's accounting software package as well as help screens on the interface. Attended a seminar on The Fundamentals of Computer Consulting in Toronto, usually offered only to full time employees.

September 1995 to
present (part time)
John Smith
Assistant to a PhD student
Assisted with all aspects of the research project. Learned how to perform testing of new developments on the system.

Summer 1994
(full time)
Goldman & Associates
Data Entry Clerk
Responsible for all data review and entry. Discovered a major accounting error that saved the company over $6,000.

Summer 1993
(full time)
Children's Learning Centre
Counsellor and Teacher
Supervised fifteen children between the ages of 4 and 9 while their parents were at work. I taught them the elementary functions of computers, using a program called Logo.

SKILLS

High level of proficiency in WordPerfect, Excel, Pascal and RBase
Speak and write English and French fluently and speak Italian well.

Heidi Adams   P. O. Box 234
(306)-355-2599   Mortlach, Sask.
Available May 1, 1996.   S0H 3E0

Education

Palliser Institute SIAST   Green River Community College
1996 - Accountancy Diploma   1978 - Associate in Applied Science
      82% average to date   Accounting Certificate
(To be completed in April 1996.)   85% average - Honour Roll

Summary of Experience

Management & Accounting	**Computer Skills**	**Special Skills**
Level 4 CGA Program	12 years experience	Business communications
8 years Office Manager	Word Perfect 6.0	Data Management
5 years Property Management	Quattro Pro 4	Property Management
6 years Job Costing	Lotus 1-2-3	Job Costing
2 years Inventory Crew Chief	dBASE III plus	Inventory Specialist
3 years Computer Consulting for	ACCPAC	
retail establishments	The General Manager	

Personal Accomplishments

Palliser Institute Achievement Award Scholarship - 1994
    $1,000.00 awarded for academic achievement and personal attributes
Southeast Regional Scholarship - 1993
    $250.00 awarded for personal attributes.
American Legion Scholarship - 1976
    $1,000.00 awarded for academic achievement and personal attributes.
Outstanding Female Athlete - Edmonds, Wash. School District #15 - 1973
    Awarded for outstanding athletic achievement and personal attributes

Community Involvement

Volunteer Work
Horse Show and Futurity Secretary
Horse Club Newsletter
Organizing Ski Races

Professional Experience

Computer Consulting

> Self Employed - working with Dacobusy Software Systems - 6/91 - Present

> Computer consulting including assisting in converting retail stores from manual systems to "The General Manager" computer system, evaluating inventory and store layout for better inventory control, and instructing in accounting techniques for better overall operations control.

Inventory Specialist

> Washington Inventory Service - Everett, Washington - 11/88 - 9/90

> Taking inventory in various locations, from small convenience stores to major department stores, by utilizing hand held data collectors and PC date compilers. Duties included training, supervising, and motivating crew members. Implemented procedures to ensure decreasing inventory count time. The Everett office consistently had less employee turnover and decreased inventory count time with greater accuracy than all other stores.

Office Manager

> Tri-Omega International   O.N. Jones Enterprises
> Dunn-Jones Construction   Skyway Park
> Company, Inc.   Coast Leasing
>   Arlington, Washington - 8/83 - 10/88

> Simultaneously took care of office management and all accounting duties for these companies. Involved with projections, job costing, and processing orders. Property management experience includes: preparing leases, tracking triple-net expenses, assessing the needs of prospective clients, and communications with banks and city officials. Before Skyway Park and Coast Leasing were sold, over 40 new businesses were housed in over 100,000 sq ft. of new pre-engineered steel buildings at the Arlington Airport.

Evening supervisor and bookkeeper

> Sno-King Ice Arena - Lynnwood, Washington - 8/79 - 7/83

> All bookkeeping duties including day-end and month-end closing, banking, evening supervising, correspondence, as well as sales, snack bar, and vending machines accounting.

The CACEE Form

As I mentioned earlier, almost all the advice I have given with respect to your resume applies equally to the CACEE form. The major difference is that the form provides you with a structure and mandatory format, as well as enabling a recruiter to quickly access the information they regard as most important. I will review the form, page by page, to highlight areas of particular concern and the different approaches that you will need to take to complete it.

Custom software

The CACEE organization now sells software that will make it very easy for you to complete the form inexpensively and efficiently. The software exactly replicates the CACEE form, and can be purchased from most school and college career centres and bookstores. It will save you endless hours of design, cutting and pasting as you try desperately to line up your typing to match the sizes of the boxes on the form. It will also make it far easier to tailor your form to the requirements of each position. It is currently available in both Windows and Macintosh environments. The Windows version requires Windows 3.0 or 3.1, 2 MB of RAM and room on a hard drive. The software is intended to be used on a stand alone computer and will not run on a network.

The first page

The company's name should be inserted in the top left hand corner. Never handwrite it in this space. Remember, you want to demonstrate it is a custom application. Handwriting the name of the company will confirm the fact that you are "applying to everyone".

Ensure that you spell the organization's name correctly. Of the nine hundred applications I received during a recent on-campus recruiting campaign, sixty-two misspelled the name of the company. That may not seem like a lot, but those 62 did not make it into the "yes" pile.

A cover letter is rarely required with a CACEE form. Be certain that your contact addresses and numbers are correct and clearly stated. And don't forget your postal code.

Get the computerized CACEE form, you can edit it each time you submit.

Colleen Rollings
Assistant Engineer, Union Gas Ltd.
University of Western Ontario
Grad '94

The position for which you are applying should be as described in the organization's advertisement. If you are not replying to an advertisement, and you really want to keep your position options open, use the space provided to refer to the last page and discuss your objectives there.

Keep in mind when the job, for which you are applying, is supposed to start before you fill in the date when you are available. Be aware that if a company is looking to hire for June 1st, for example, and you can only start on September 7th, you'll be eliminated from consideration, no matter how good your application is. Do your research first. If you are really interested in this particular job or company, can you make yourself available? If it's a vacation that's in your way, can it be rearranged? If it's because of school commitments, indicate this clearly on your form. With any luck you will have gotten to know someone from the organization during the process with whom you can discuss your dilemma.

You'd be amazed at how much more accommodating people can be if they have gotten to know you and have been impressed. They will treat you differently, and be far more flexible if they know who you are.

Willing to accept employment anywhere in Canada?

Again, research will help you complete this question correctly. If the organization has locations across the country and you are willing to relocate, list your preferred locations. If the organization only has operations in Calgary and Vancouver, listing your preferred locations as Toronto, Edmonton and Calgary will not result in the desired response. If these are your preferred locations, consider whether you should be applying to the organization. If you are still exploring your options you should state that Calgary is your preferred location with respect to this particular employer. Think of the situation from the employer's perspective. At the initial application stage, if they are looking for people for their Calgary location and Calgary is your third choice, should they select you if you really would prefer to work elsewhere? It is unlikely that they will if there are equally qualified applicants whose first choice of location is Calgary.

Two pieces of advice with respect to locations. First, do your research and find out where an organization's offices are located, then decide where you are willing to work. Armed with this information, complete the form as I

In filling out ACCIS forms, write from your heart, not from a "what they want you to say" point of view.

Rachelle Kowal
Business Analyst, TransAlta
Utilities Corporation, University
of Saskatchewan Grad '95

have described remembering that if you say you are willing to accept employment elsewhere, you have to fill in preferences. Many students either indicate that they are willing, but then fail to fill in any selections. If it really doesn't matter to you, leave it blank. Others applicants read this second part of the form as preferred "other" locations and as a result they fail to enter their primary choice location at all. Your first choice location should always be number one.

Education

You should start with your current institution and proceed in reverse chronological order all the way back to your high school. Ensure that you have spelled the names of the institutions correctly and that you describe your discipline, program, degree, diploma or certificate accurately. Don't make a mistake in dates. Errors will cause confusion and doubt which you cannot afford.

Skills and achievements

Unlike a resume, where it is up to you to determine the amount of space you use to describe your skills and achievements, a CACEE form allocates a fixed amount of space, thus predetermining how much information you can give. Be selective. State those skills and achievements that are most relevant to the particular position. Using the CACEE form software will enable you to adapt each application to the specific job skill set. For example, if your computer skills are crucial to the position, you should clearly state all your relevant software application skills and your knowledge of hardware. If it is a far less important part of the job, you may want to limit your comments to just your primary skills. If you have too many relevant skills and achievements, the best place to discuss them is on the last page of the form, there, you can elaborate. This allows you to simply state the facts on the first page, then use the last page to illustrate their relevancy to the position. Skills you might include are:

Languages	Licences
Computer Knowledge	Accreditations
Technical Skills	

GPA and marks

The requirements of this section are clear. Many resume reviewers will simply discard a resume and not look beyond this first page if the marks are below what they accept. If you feel you may fall into this category but have a legitimate explanation, make sure you clearly indicate the fact. Use the last page of the form to do so.

This is also the appropriate place to indicate your standing in class, if you know it and you think it is relevant.

Work experience

Even more so than in the freeform resume, your space is limited, so you do not have room to explain positions that do not require explanation. Elaborate only on your relevant skills and achievements. Be sure to indicate clearly which jobs were full time or part time. If they were part time, remember to state the average number of hours you worked per week.

Extracurricular activities

Once again your space is limited, so you will want to use it wisely. Stick to your most relevant skills and the activities you think will be most impressive to the organization. If working in a team is a crucial skill for the position, you'll want to highlight your team skills and successes. If leadership is essential, the activities related to any leadership positions you've held are important. Remember, there is no need to mention the name of an organization in which you were involved if it indicates race, ancestry, place of origin, colour, ethnic background, citizenship, creed, sexual orientation, age, marital status, family status, political beliefs or disabilities. You can simply mention the nature of the organization, the position you held, and your primary responsibilities. For example:

> I was the President of the Youth division of a political party from 1991 to 1994. I chaired all the Committees and was directly responsible for fund raising and recruiting new members.

> I was a religious instruction teacher from 1988 to 1993. I set the weekly curriculum, and taught and motivated the twenty children in my class.

Don't leave completing the ACCIS form to the last minute! It takes a long time to fill out the form correctly.

Cindy Stephenson
Director, Faculty of Management, Placement Centre, University of Manitoba

I have been deeply involved in my community for the past ten years. We oriented new immigrants to Canada and taught them English and French.

Career objectives

You should begin by stating your overall long term career objective, then follow it with your short term objective, tailored to the specific position and organization to which you are sending your form. For example:

Long Term Objective

To be a project leader in a computer consulting company.

Short Term Objective

To be a systems analyst in a computer consulting firm and to learn consulting methodology and the manufacturing environments in which you specialize.

It should never be as vague as "I am seeking a trainee position with your company". Your career objectives should be as specific as possible. An even more meaningless and yet, all too common objective, "I am seeking any position that will utilize my knowledge".

It is the ideal opportunity to show the organization that you have an in depth understanding of the position for which you are applying and a sound knowledge of the company. A generic career objective is transparent to recruiters and won't score points.

Additional information

The students I interviewed and who responded to the survey felt that this was the most difficult part of the form to complete.

I have seen many forms where the entire page is filled and others where this page is left blank. I believe that your objective in completing this page should be to pull your application together by ensuring that the following three questions are answered:

Why are you interested in the organization?
Why are you perfectly suited for the position?
Why should the organization choose you for an interview?

The space provided allows you to give examples in each case and to further illustrate and highlight information you have previously mentioned. It provides you with the chance to explain how the skills you've acquired will be useful on the job, and how your extracurricular activities have allowed you to grow and develop as a person. It also provides you with a further opportunity to demonstrate your knowledge of the company and the position for which you are applying.

Do not feel obligated to fill the page. You do not need to discuss each of your jobs and activities. The important thing is to tie your application together by making it warm, friendly and interesting, and to distinguish yourself from the other applicants, making the reader absolutely long to meet you.

The sign-off

During each recruiting campaign, approximately fifteen percent of applicants, for some inexplicable reason, do not sign or date the form. It shows that you do not care about details and that you cannot follow simple written instructions. Sign and date the form.

References

I am often asked by students who they should give as references. The first rule is that it must be someone who will say positive things about you. I recently called a reference who said "I am not sure why she gave me as a reference, we didn't really work well together". He went on to add "I suppose she did not have anyone else". Hardly a glowing endorsement!

The second is that you must choose someone who will want to take the time to answer the calls and will sound enthusiastic. I recently attempted, unsuccessfully, to reach a referee. Frustrated, I left a message stating who I was and why I was calling. The person never returned my call, leaving me with a very negative feeling about the candidate, even though nothing negative had been said. Always ensure the referee knows you are giving out their name as a reference. It is also a good idea to call them and let them know that a specific company will be calling, so that they can be on the lookout for a message.

Wherever possible, make the referee someone who will impress the recruiter. Chances are greater that a positive reference from an impressive source will carry more weight.

Consider the following people to use as references:

Managers and supervisors for whom you have worked or are working
Professors
Members of the clergy
Community leaders
High School teachers
People in the industry

Always remember to give their names, titles, business addresses, phone numbers and, unless it is obvious, your relationship with the referee.

CACEE APPLICATION FOR EMPLOYMENT

APPROVED BY

CACEE·ACSEE

- ◉ PERMANENT
- ○ SUMMER
- ○ CO-OP
- ○ INTERNSHIP

NAME OF COMPANY	POSITION(S) SOUGHT	NAME OF EDUCATIONAL INSTITUTION
Wright, Auger & Harrow	Audit Trainee	University of Toronto

GENERAL INFORMATION

SURNAME	GIVEN NAME(S)
Smith	Dora

ADDRESS until __permanent__

No.	Street	City	Prov./State	E-mail
			ON	
2802	Davis Rd.	Toronto	Postal Code	Tel.
			M8C 5M7	(416)-555-6502

PERMANENT ADDRESS IN CANADA IF DIFFERENT FROM ABOVE

No.	Street	City	Prov./State	E-mail
			Postal Code	Tel.

ARE YOU LEGALLY ELIGIBLE TO ACCEPT EMPLOYMENT IN CANADA?
DOCUMENTARY EVIDENCE MAY BE REQUESTED AFTER A JOB OFFER IS MADE.　　◉ YES　　○ NO

WHEN ARE YOU AVAILABLE TO START WORK?	WOULD YOU ACCEPT EMPLOYMENT ANYWHERE IN CANADA?　○ YES　◉ NO
Spring 1996	PREFERRED LOCATION(S) 1. Toronto 2. Montreal 3.

EDUCATION

ENTER NAME(S) OF POST SECONDARY AND SECONDARY INSTITUTIONS ATTENDED, BEGIN WITH MOST RECENT INSTITUTION ATTENDED	FACULTY, DEPARTMENT DIVISION OR SCHOOL	DISCIPLINE OR PROGRAMME (MAJOR)	DEGREE/ DIPLOMA CERTIFICATE	DATE OBTAINED OR EXPECTED
University of Toronto	Commerce	Accounting / Marketing	Bachelor of Commerce	May 1996
Lawrence Park Collegiate			High School Certificate	June 1992

RELEVANT SKILLS AND ACHIEVEMENTS: THIS MAY INCLUDE SCHOLARSHIP(S) AND AWARD(S), COMPUTER LITERACY, LANGUAGE SKILLS (LEVEL OF FLUENCY, SPOKEN AND WRITTEN) AND OTHER RELEVANT SKILLS.

*Received a full scholarship for the 1994-1995 academic year.
*Placed on the Dean's List in 1993, 1994, 1995.
*Graduated Lawrence Park Collegiate with honours.
*Won an award at Summer Sun Camp as "Best New Counsellor".
*Proficient at WordPerfect, Word and Excel.
*Good knowledge of ACCPAC and FAST.
*Working knowledge of French.

PLEASE INDICATE YOUR GRADE POINT AVERAGE (G.P.A.) FOR YOUR MOST RECENTLY COMPLETED ACADEMIC YEAR
__3.67__ ON A SCALE OF __4.3__ (PERCENTAGE OR LETTER EQUIVALENT _____).

PLEASE INDICATE YOUR GRADE POINT AVERAGE (G.P.A.) FOR ALL COURSES COMPLETED TO DATE (CUMULATIVE AVERAGE)
__3.7__ ON A SCALE OF __4.3__ (PERCENTAGE OR LETTER EQUIVALENT _____).

WORK EXPERIENCE

PLEASE LIST ALL EMPLOYMENT STARTING WITH MOST RECENT EMPLOYER

Robbins & Richard   FROM May 1994   TO August 1994
NAME OF ORGANIZATION

Markham   Ontario   Summer Student
CITY   PROVINCE/STATE   JOB TITLE

DUTIES: ☒ SUMMER

Performed audits and inventory counts at Robbins & Richard's   ☐ PART TIME
clients. Learned and used ACCPAC, FAST and Excel software.   # of hours/week: _____
Received a 10/10 end of summer evaluation, the highest ever
given to a summer student.   ☐ CO-OP

                                                   ☐ FULL-TIME

                                                   ☐ INTERNSHIP

Grant Jewellers   FROM Nov. 1993   TO present
NAME OF ORGANIZATION

Toronto   Ontario   Assistant Manager
CITY   PROVINCE/STATE   JOB TITLE

DUTIES: ☐ SUMMER

Designed a new system to automatically update inventory   ☒ PART TIME
records from invoices, prepared daily bank deposits and   # of hours/week: 15
balanced the cash on a daily basis. I also developed a new
strategy for displaying merchandise, whereby annual sales   ☐ CO-OP
increased by 12.5%. Promoted from salesperson to present
position after twelve months.   ☐ FULL-TIME

                                                   ☐ INTERNSHIP

Investment Strategies Inc.   FROM Summer 1992   TO Summer 1993
NAME OF ORGANIZATION

Toronto   Ontario   Bookkeeper
CITY   PROVINCE/STATE   JOB TITLE

DUTIES: ☒ SUMMER

During the summers of 1992 and 1993, I was responsible for   ☐ PART TIME
preparing and recording journal entries, reconciling bank   # of hours/week: _____
statements and assisting the auditor with the preparation of
working papers for the fiscal year end.   ☐ CO-OP

                                                   ☐ FULL-TIME

                                                   ☐ INTERNSHIP

Summer Sun Camp   FROM June 1991   TO Aug. 1991
NAME OF ORGANIZATION

Toronto   Ontario   Senior Camp Counsellor
CITY   PROVINCE/STATE   JOB TITLE

DUTIES: ☒ SUMMER

For eight weeks, I was responsible for the safety of ten,   ☐ PART TIME
twelve year old girls. I designed and co-ordinated daily and   # of hours/week: _____
evening programs. In addition, I evaluated new staff on camp
policies and procedures. Promoted from Junior Counsellor.   ☐ CO-OP

                                                   ☐ FULL-TIME

                                                   ☐ INTERNSHIP

EXTRACURRICULAR ACTIVITIES

INDICATE YOUR EXTRACURRICULAR ACTIVITIES INCLUDING CLASS OR CAMPUS OFFICES HELD, VOLUNTEER EXPERIENCE, MEMBERSHIPS IN CLUBS OR ORGANIZATIONS, LEADERSHIP ROLES, SPORTS ACTIVITIES, HOBBIES, ETC. (YOU ARE NOT REQUIRED TO MENTION THE NAMES OF ORGANIZATIONS THAT INDICATE RACE, ANCESTRY, PLACE OF ORIGIN, COLOUR, ETHNIC ORIGIN, CITIZENSHIP, CREED, SEX, SEXUAL ORIENTATION, AGE, MARITAL STATUS, FAMILY STATUS, POLITICAL BELIEFS OR DISABILITIES).

I have always prided myself on achieving high standards in my studies. However, merely doing well in school does not satisfy my need for achievement. I am also involved in many extracurricular activites.

I am currently a contributing writer for The Varsity (school newspaper). I write bi-weekly articles based on student surveys. I conduct the surveys on campus and then write a report on my findings. I have also been involved with student council elections. I was the campaign manager for a candidate who ran for President (who ended up winning!). My duties included cold calling, designing posters, making speeches on his behalf and encouraging other students to become involved.

In high school, I was yearbook coordinator. As editor, I had many responsibilities and the 125 graduates counted on my leadership to produce the book. I was responsible for appointing staff, designing layouts and fundraising. This position was very challenging and took up most of my free time. The yearbook was a tremendous success.

CAREER OBJECTIVES

INDICATE YOUR CAREER OBJECTIVES. THIS MAY INCLUDE FIELD(S) OF INTEREST AND JOB PREFERENCE(S).

I would like to begin my career as an Audit Trainee in a challenging and stimulating environment where I will have the opportunity to put my theoretical knowledge to use. My long term goal is to become a Partner in a firm of Chartered Accountants.

Dora's CACEE form

ELABORATE ON THE FACTUAL MATERIAL ALREADY PRESENTED AND SHOW HOW THIS EXPERIENCE (EDUCATIONAL, EXTRA-CURRICULAR AND WORK) IS RELEVANT TO THE POSITION, ORGANIZATION AND/OR FIELD OF WORK FOR WHICH YOU ARE APPLYING.

I am a person who is never satisfied until I have done my best. My scholastic background is a perfect example. I graduated from high school with very high grades. At the University of Toronto, I continued my pursuit of excellence. My hard work has not gone unrewarded. Not only have I earned a place on the Dean's List each year but I also received a full scholarship for the 1994/1995 academic year.

Knowing early on that my goal was to become a Chartered Accountant, I have tried over the years to gain as much practical experience as possible. Working as a bookkeeper for Investment Strategies Inc., I learned how well suited I was for the accounting profession.

The summer I spent at Robbins & Richard gave me the opportunity to learn even more about the profession. I worked on audits and learned to use accounting software. Moreover, I became familiar with the daily operations of a large accounting firm. Having worked for a large organization in this industry confirmed my interest in the field of accounting. I received an offer from Robbins & Richard upon graduation. I have not accepted it however as I would really like to work for Wright, Auger & Harrow.

I have proven experience in the field of accounting and possess the necessary skills required to deal with the challenges at Wright, Auger & Harrow. I am highly motivated and success oriented. I believe I have the qualifications to make an excellent accountant.

Thank you for your time and consideration.

I UNDERSTAND THAT ANY OMISSION OR MISREPRESENTATION WITH RESPECT TO THIS INFORMATION MAY BE CAUSE FOR DENIAL OR IMMEDIATE TERMINATION OF EMPLOYMENT.

January 16, 1996.
DATE

SIGNATURE

CACEE APPLICATION FOR EMPLOYMENT

APPROVED BY

CACEE · ACSEE

- ● PERMANENT
- ○ SUMMER
- ○ CO-OP
- ○ INTERNSHIP

NAME OF COMPANY	POSITION(S) SOUGHT	NAME OF EDUCATIONAL INSTITUTION
Communications Canada Inc.	Public Relations Consultant	University of Manitoba

GENERAL INFORMATION

SURNAME	GIVEN NAME(S)
Thomas	Derek

ADDRESS until <u>permanent</u>

No.	Street	City	Prov./State	E-mail
1658	Beacon St. #3A	Winnipeg	MB Postal Code R2M 8T3	Tel. (204)-555-1921

PERMANENT ADDRESS IN CANADA IF DIFFERENT FROM ABOVE

No.	Street	City	Prov./State	E-mail
			Postal Code	Tel.

ARE YOU LEGALLY ELIGIBLE TO ACCEPT EMPLOYMENT IN CANADA?
DOCUMENTARY EVIDENCE MAY BE REQUESTED AFTER A JOB OFFER IS MADE.   ● YES   ○ NO

WHEN ARE YOU AVAILABLE TO START WORK?	WOULD YOU ACCEPT EMPLOYMENT ANYWHERE IN CANADA? ● YES ○ NO
May 1996	PREFERRED LOCATION(S) 1. Winnipeg 2. Edmonton 3. Vancouver

EDUCATION

ENTER NAME(S) OF POST SECONDARY AND SECONDARY INSTITUTIONS ATTENDED, BEGIN WITH MOST RECENT INSTITUTION ATTENDED	FACULTY, DEPARTMENT DIVISION OR SCHOOL	DISCIPLINE OR PROGRAMME (MAJOR)	DEGREE/ DIPLOMA CERTIFICATE	DATE OBTAINED OR EXPECTED
University of Manitoba	Faculty of Arts	Labour Studies	Bachelor of Arts	May 1996
John Taylor Collegiate			High School Certificate	June 1992

RELEVANT SKILLS AND ACHIEVEMENTS: THIS MAY INCLUDE SCHOLARSHIP(S) AND AWARD(S), COMPUTER LITERACY, LANGUAGE SKILLS (LEVEL OF FLUENCY, SPOKEN AND WRITTEN) AND OTHER RELEVANT SKILLS.

Hands-on experience with WordPerfect 6.1, dBASE and Lotus 1-2-3 software.

Fluently bilingual in English and French.

Red Cross Nationals Certificate.

PLEASE INDICATE YOUR GRADE POINT AVERAGE (G.P.A.) FOR YOUR MOST RECENTLY COMPLETED ACADEMIC YEAR
__3.1__ ON A SCALE OF __4.5__ (PERCENTAGE OR LETTER EQUIVALENT _____).
PLEASE INDICATE YOUR GRADE POINT AVERAGE (G.P.A.) FOR ALL COURSES COMPLETED TO DATE (CUMULATIVE AVERAGE)
__3.1__ ON A SCALE OF __4.5__ (PERCENTAGE OR LETTER EQUIVALENT _____).

WORK EXPERIENCE

PLEASE LIST ALL EMPLOYMENT STARTING WITH MOST RECENT EMPLOYER

Dr. Jacob Small
NAME OF ORGANIZATION

FROM June 1994   TO present

Winnipeg   Manitoba
CITY   PROVINCE/STATE

Receptionist
JOB TITLE

DUTIES:

Developed a new database system using dBASE whereby the doctor and hygienist saved considerable time retrieving patient records. Aside from my duties as a receptionist, I am the liaison with insurance companies, ensuring our clients' claims are properly processed.

☐ SUMMER
☒ PART TIME
   # of hours/week: 12
☐ CO-OP
☐ FULL-TIME
☐ INTERNSHIP

Shoe Bazaar
NAME OF ORGANIZATION

FROM Sept. 1993   TO present

Winnipeg   Manitoba
CITY   PROVINCE/STATE

Shift Manager
JOB TITLE

DUTIES:

Responsible for opening and closing the store and preparing the weekly work schedule. Supervised and trained new employees. Promoted from stock person to salesperson after just three months. Promoted from salesperson to shift manager after one year.

☐ SUMMER
☒ PART TIME
   # of hours/week: 20
☐ CO-OP
☐ FULL-TIME
☐ INTERNSHIP

Fredericton Community Pool
NAME OF ORGANIZATION

FROM June 1993   TO Sept. 1993

Winnipeg   Manitoba
CITY   PROVINCE/STATE

Lifeguard
JOB TITLE

DUTIES:

Worked as a lifeguard where I planned activities for children, organized a first-aid course for pool members and conducted tests on chlorine levels of the pool each day.

☒ SUMMER
☐ PART TIME
   # of hours/week: _____
☐ CO-OP
☐ FULL-TIME
☐ INTERNSHIP

_____
NAME OF ORGANIZATION

FROM _____   TO _____

_____
CITY   PROVINCE/STATE

_____
JOB TITLE

DUTIES:

☐ SUMMER
☐ PART TIME
   # of hours/week: _____
☐ CO-OP
☐ FULL-TIME
☐ INTERNSHIP

EXTRACURRICULAR ACTIVITIES

INDICATE YOUR EXTRACURRICULAR ACTIVITIES INCLUDING CLASS OR CAMPUS OFFICES HELD, VOLUNTEER EXPERIENCE, MEMBERSHIPS IN CLUBS OR ORGANIZATIONS, LEADERSHIP ROLES, SPORTS ACTIVITIES, HOBBIES, ETC. (YOU ARE NOT REQUIRED TO MENTION THE NAMES OF ORGANIZATIONS THAT INDICATE RACE, ANCESTRY, PLACE OF ORIGIN, COLOUR, ETHNIC ORIGIN, CITIZENSHIP, CREED, SEX, SEXUAL ORIENTATION, AGE, MARITAL STATUS, FAMILY STATUS, POLITICAL BELIEFS OR DISABILITIES).

1994 - present: Involved in fundraising for the swim team at the University of Manitoba.

1992 - present: Captain of the Manitoba Bisons (Intercollegiate) Hockey Team.

1991 - present: Active member of the intercollegiate swim team.

1991: Taught the Red Cross National Certificate course.

1991: Taught mentally challenged children how to ice skate.

CAREER OBJECTIVES

INDICATE YOUR CAREER OBJECTIVES. THIS MAY INCLUDE FIELD(S) OF INTEREST AND JOB PREFERENCE(S).

My objective is to begin a career in the Communications industry in which I would make use of my education and work experience.

In the long term, I would like to be a Director of Public Relations where I could be responsible for corporate communications for a large organization.

ADDITIONAL INFORMATION

ELABORATE ON THE FACTUAL MATERIAL ALREADY PRESENTED AND SHOW HOW THIS EXPERIENCE (EDUCATIONAL, EXTRA-CURRICULAR AND WORK) IS RELEVANT TO THE POSITION, ORGANIZATION AND/OR FIELD OF WORK FOR WHICH YOU ARE APPLYING.

Being Captain of the University of Manitoba's Hockey Team gives me the opportunity to learn many of the skills that are necessary for a job in the Communications field. I have learned organization, communication and interpersonal skills. It has also given me an opportunity to deal extensively with the media. As well, having team members from all regions of Canada has opened my eyes to new cultures and different people. It has also taught me the importance of team work. Each week, I am responsible for leading the practices and motivating the team. In addition, I am responsible for managing the team's finances.

In the winter of 1991, I taught mentally challenged children to ice skate. It was by far the most challenging experience I have ever had. Even when the children were unable to make it around the rink without falling, the smiles on their faces and their desire to succeed never disappeared. This taught me to never lose my determination and to believe in myself.

My studies at the University of Manitoba, coupled with all the valuable skills I have learned through extracurricular activities have given me the skills that are necessary for a career in the Public Relations Consulting field.

I UNDERSTAND THAT ANY OMISSION OR MISREPRESENTATION WITH RESPECT TO THIS INFORMATION MAY BE CAUSE FOR DENIAL OR IMMEDIATE TERMINATION OF EMPLOYMENT.

March 3, 1996.
DATE

SIGNATURE

Here is a last minute CACEE form checklist of details that definitely make a difference to recruiters:

If you have used a word processor, have you ensured that all the boxes are lined up and the final copy is clean and neat?

Is your name, address and telephone number (fax and E-mail, if applicable) clearly shown at the top of the first page?

Are the dates shown for the schools you attended correct?

Have you clearly indicated your level of proficiency for each of the languages you speak and write?

Have you clearly indicated your level of proficiency for the computer software programs for which you have indicated experience and understanding?

Have you provided your marks in the appropriate places on the form?

Have you clearly shown what you accomplished and what you learned in each job you held?

Have you emphasized duties that show your specific skills and accomplishments and avoided those that don't?

Have you eliminated all erroneous information that does not directly apply to the position for which you are applying?

Is it interesting to read?

Is it visually pleasing?

Have you excluded all unnecessary information such as social insurance number, height, weight and marital status?

Did you use action verbs to describe your duties, accomplishments and involvement?

Have you checked all spelling and grammar? Twice? Three times?

Has a third party reviewed your resume to ensure that there are absolutely no spelling or grammar errors?

Did you sign and date the form?

If you have photocopied the form, have the photocopies come out clearly and cleanly?

If you have included a transcript of your courses and marks, has this been clearly and cleanly photocopied?

Be specific with respect to career objective – state your interests – not 'a job where I can apply my skills'.

Sue Riddell
Manager, Employment & Staffing,
DuPont Canada Inc.

93

Action Verbs with Pizzazz

Throughout the resume, use strong action verbs that powerfully describe your work experience, career objectives, and accomplishments. The more powerful the words you use, the more the tasks come alive and the reader will be able to envisage you performing them. They will reduce your generic use of words and phrases such as:

did	was responsible for
gave	placed
helped	took

Examples of words you should use can be found in Appendix I at the end of the book.

Power Words and Phrases

Appendix II contains a list of "power" words and phrases you may want to consider using in your resume and cover letters. In each case, recruiters will expect you to prove these skills and attributes with examples.

Preparing for Interviews

6

Performing at Your Peak

To perform at your very best during interviews, you have to be both mentally and physically prepared. In this chapter, I will walk you through the steps necessary to ensure that you perform to the best of your ability each time.

The time between your selection for a first interview and the actual event is usually both exciting and anxiety filled. A proper, well-planned strategy will ensure that you peak for each interview.

Your "Best Qualities Card"

It is essential that you have an interview game plan. These three steps will help you put it into action.

1. Analyse the job requirements in detail.

2. List your best qualities, character traits and accomplishments as they relate to those job requirements. Don't use a generic card. The basic information will stay the same, but just as with your cover letters and resume, each card must be tailored to the position.

3. Keep in mind the question "Why should we hire you?" as you prepare your "Best Qualities Card". This card contains a summary of all the information you absolutely must tell the interviewers. Know that the interview cannot end until you have told the interviewer every reason on the card "why they should hire you".

Mentally eliminate each item from your list as it is discussed. If you are left with anything you have absolutely not been able to fit into an answer, take one of two approaches. Wait until an appropriate moment near the end of the interview and tell them that there is one more piece of relevant information that you want to share with them or wait until they ask you if you have any questions. Reply that you do but mention you have one further thing to add.

You may be the most qualified person for the job, but if you don't market yourself effectively in the first interview, you won't be the successful candidate.

Ann-Marie Elliott
Placement Services Coordinator,
York University

First Interviews

These are often held on-campus but if they are not, the advice with respect to preparing for interviews held at an organization's offices will apply.

Career centres' and organizations' methods of informing you that you have been selected for an interview vary considerably. So I suggest visiting the Career Centre at least three times a week (every day would be even better) and ensuring that your telephone answering system is in place to check for any correspondence regarding a job. If you are relying on an electronic device, be sure that it is on and working. If it's the people you live with who will be answering the phone, make sure they know what you want them to say and do. Ask them to be professional and take full, clear messages.

The primary reason for constantly monitoring the communication system is because most organizations will post a list of people selected for a first interview and the times and dates that they will be conducting the interviews. Students' selection of a time slot is usually done on a first-come-first-served basis and you want to have as wide a choice as possible.

Personal Grooming

No one I know ever got a job because of how well they dressed. Many people, however, are ultimately eliminated from contention because of how poorly they dressed. Looking the part of a successful candidate will do a lot for your self confidence and, believe me, everyone can do with a shot of additional confidence early in the process.

The most important advice I can give you is to always give yourself enough time before each event to check your grooming. There will always be a washroom available, so give yourself a ten minute buffer and take the time to do last minute touch-ups.

The research you have done into the industry and the organization is crucial and will ultimately dictate what you should wear. But there are general guidelines to be followed:

Lack of preparation which results in a poor interview really turns me off a candidate.

Sue Riddell
Manager, Employment & Staffing,
DuPont Canada Inc.

96

General dress guidelines

When in doubt, take the more conservative approach. You're always better off overdressed than underdressed.

Ensure that everything you wear is clean and well pressed. You do not need to carry a briefcase. A portfolio with a copy of your resume and/or CACEE form and a clean note pad are sufficient.

In bad weather, where you are forced to wear boots or overshoes, always take an extra pair of shoes into which you can change. Wet, soiled boots are unprofessional and at company visits, can ruin floors and carpets.

Men's dress

1. You may as well think positively and buy that first suit and tie if you don't already own them. Suits should be navy blue or charcoal. Stay away from brown whenever possible. A thin stripe or check is acceptable in almost all situations. If a sports jacket and tie are the norm for your industry, conservative dark colours are once again suggested.

2. Ties should be worn, even if the majority of people in the industry don't wear them. Ties have become more flamboyant in the last couple of years. Steer clear of the fashion ties with messages or outrageous colour combinations. Just make sure they complement the rest of your outfit. Remember the rule that whichever tie knot you use, the bottom of your tie should be just in line with the top of your belt. Leather ties or western string-ties should not be worn. If in doubt, get advice.

3. Shoes should be black or burgundy, lace ups or loafers with a thin regular sole. Loafers should not be covered with decorations and buckles. Boots should never be worn unless the interview includes a site visit where this is the norm. Even then, I would suggest bringing a change of footwear for the office portion of the visit.

4. Your socks must coordinate with your pants, not your shirt, which means white is out. Plain colours are preferred but a small pattern is certainly acceptable. Make sure they are able to stay up high enough to cover your leg in case your pants rise. There's nothing more unattractive than bare legs in a professional setting.

Be prepared, practice, preferably in a mock interview at the Career Centre or with friends and family.

Ann-Marie Elliott
Placement Services Coordinator,
York University

5. Shirts should be white or light colours, preferably gray or blue. A light coloured shirt with a white collar and cuffs is acceptable. For those seeking entry-level positions, the heavy-stripe, white collar, power shirt is a little too much and should be avoided.

6. Debate still rages on about beards, moustaches and hair. My best advice is to do your research and see what the norm is in your industry. Be warned however, that many interviewers are opposed to facial hair and long hair. I know this seems unfair, but it is a fact of life in recruiting. My main advice is make sure you look neat, clean, well groomed and very recently shaven.

7. Earrings. Leave these to the female candidates. I have not encountered many recruiters who are comfortable with this, so no earrings, please.

8. Jewellery should be kept to a minimum and be unobtrusive.

9. Cologne and aftershave should be subtle.

Women's dress

This is far more complex than guidelines for men because of the wider variety of choices.

The question of a dress versus a suit, and the acceptability of pants is a matter of personal opinion. Individual recruiter's opinion, that is. Unfortunately, there are no hard and fast rules that I can give you that would make my life, and consequently your life, easy. It is almost impossible to get two recruiters to agree, so giving you advice that will work for all situations is impossible. Once again, it's up to you to do the research and find out exactly what is acceptable in your particular field. Having said that, please take all of the following advice bearing that in mind:

1. Skirts, jackets, pants and suits should be well-tailored. They should be dry cleaned and pressed regularly throughout the process. While not suggesting you stick to basic black, blue and dark gray, I do suggest that if you are going to wear bright colours you have more than one outfit. Recruiters will remember that exceptional outfit. So if you have to wear it again, you may feel self conscious. If you plan to buy new clothes, remember the value of buying clothes that will mix and match.

2. Blouses should be of high quality and freshly pressed before each event in the process.

3. Make up and perfume should be as subtle as possible.

4. Shoes should be pumps and the height of the heel should be comfortable to you but certainly not the stiletto variety. Remember, you are probably going to have to do a fair amount of standing and walking, so comfort is important. Shoes being worn for the first time often cause problems, so unless you want to limp through the entire process, break in new shoes. Boots and open-toed shoes should not be worn.

5. Hosiery should be worn. Definitely not socks, but flesh tones or sheer black are recommended. Forget the patterns or seams. I suggest bringing along an extra pair of hose just in case of a run on the way to the interview. Torn stockings are very unprofessional.

6. Jewellery should, like your make-up and perfume, be subtle and be used to complement your outfit. If you are in a fairly conservative industry, use it to make your look more professional. A sophisticated broach will go a long way to making plain clothes look the part. If you don't have one, borrow. If you are in an arts or fashion industry, use your accessories to enhance the look.

7. Advice on hair is straight forward. Keep it off your face and make sure it looks under control at all times. In the winter months avoid hat hair.

What is the Best Time for an Interview?

This is a common question with an easy answer. What time slots are still available? What time of the day are you at your very best?

Choose that slot for your interview. So many students spend hours trying to determine what will be the best time for the interviewer, when he or she will be at their friendliest. Don't waste your time. Unless you know the interviewers well (and you probably don't), it's not worth speculating on their best time of day or mood. The one factor over which you do have control is you, so go ahead and select your best time. Keep in mind that you will probably need at least one hour each before and after the interview, so give yourself sufficient leeway when setting up your schedule. I also suggest that you schedule no more than two first interviews on one day.

Know your resume backwards and forwards. Don't be afraid to bring out a point you feel is important, if they don't.

Shelly Broad
Financial Forecast Analyst,
Union Gas Ltd.,
Wilfrid Laurier University Grad '94

Researching Interviewers/Employers

Finding out who your interviewers will be is far more difficult than researching potential employers but very useful if you can get the lowdown. It is helpful to know their interview style and the types of questions they usually ask ahead of time. Fortunately, most interviewers have a consistent interview style and knowing something about it will make your preparation easier and more focussed. The best way to find out who will be doing the interview is to ask the organization representatives at the Career Fair or at their information session. Or inquire at the Career Centre.

Your best source of information about the interviewers is someone who has already gone through the interview process with the organization.

Site Inspections

It is a very good idea to visit the interview location before the actual interview takes place. If it's taking place at the Career Centre or in a building with which you are familiar, there is no need to check out the location. If you are not familiar with the location, make certain you know exactly where it is and the easiest way to get there. If possible, try to get a feel for the rooms where the interviews take place. Even if you just spend a minute in the room, it will feel a little more familiar when you visit it later. Spend ten minutes and it will almost feel like home.

Arrival time

Ideally, you should arrive at the interview location no more than ten minutes before the scheduled start time. Spend the next five minutes in the washroom making last minute adjustments to your physical appearance. Now you only have five minutes to kill. Try to relax if that's at all possible. If the waiting area is filled with other anxious students waiting for their interviews, try to avoid it until the last possible moment. The prevailing atmosphere will only heighten your anxiety. Spend the time thinking about the particular position for which you are being interviewed. Reread those key factors on your "Best Qualities Card". Keep thinking about the skills required for the position and how you are going to convince the interviewers you're the best candidate.

Being late

There are always circumstances beyond our control that cause us to be late. I advise you, and everyone else will too, not to be late. I am sure you will do everything in your power to be on time. However, just in case, here is some advice if you are running late.

Call the Career Centre immediately if it's an interview that has been arranged through them and it is being held at your institution. If it's an off-campus interview, call the organization directly to let them know you may be late. Forewarned is forearmed and they may be able to adjust their schedule. If they are running late, you may still make it on time. If you are rushing through the campus, stop at a pay phone and call ahead. If your car is stuck in traffic, pull over and call to let someone know. Do everything you can to let them know you are concerned about the fact that you are late or are going to be late. Do not let the perspiration streaming down your brow be the only indication that you're in trouble.

Just before the interview

The time has arrived. Make sure you can get up from your seat without stumbling and that your right hand is free. When you first see the interviewers, be ready to shake their hands immediately. If you are meeting with two people, shake the hand of the person who first addresses you, then the other.

Getting comfortable

The seats provided in interview rooms are generally not particularly comfortable. Realize that you are going to have to be in one for at least thirty minutes and try to sit comfortably. Relaxing your hands and shoulders usually works wonders. You are not frozen into your first position so if you're uncomfortable, shift you body to another position.

Now you are ready to begin. Enjoy yourself, because if you do, the interviewers will too and you're half way there.

The kickoff

It's in everyone's best interest to quickly establish a rapport. If you have met the interviewers before, you have a distinct advantage. Discuss something of mutual interest. The Career Fair, their information session or a comment or two about the event where you met is always appropriate and will quickly establish a warm atmosphere. They may choose to discuss the weather, the room they are in or the recruiting process. If you have a particularly interesting or unusual aspect to your resume, this may be discussed. If you have a pilot's licence, spent a summer backpacking in Mongolia or if you worked in the Arctic for a year, be ready to discuss it as soon as the interview begins. Remember that the objective is to get everyone in the room relaxed and comfortable with one another. Use the opportunity to calm down, not to make yourself more anxious.

Questions you may want to ask

The following is a list of questions you'll want to ask company representatives if you have not been able to find out the information from your research or the information they distributed.

> Could you please describe a typical day on the job?
>
> What type of training does this organization offer?
>
> When do the training programs begin?
>
> What is the typical career path for position X?
>
> Is the workload fairly steady all year-round? If not, what are the busy times?
>
> Will I have a chance to meet my co-workers?
>
> Are there specific skills or experience that are beneficial in helping someone do well in this job?
>
> Do most managers have advanced degrees? If so, which ones?
>
> When will my first job performance evaluation take place?
>
> How often will I be evaluated?
>
> Are there any bonuses associated with job performance?
>
> Do people get promoted based on performance or seniority?
>
> To whom will I report?
>
> Does your company anticipate changing its current structure in the near future?
>
> Will (a political event) impact the organization in any way?
>
> How many new graduates do you typically hire each year?
>
> How frequently do you relocate entry level employees?

How much travel will I be expected to do in a typical year?

Is it possible to transfer from one division to another?

How much input does a new employee have in decision making in the first year?

What is the average age of top management?

What is the average time to get to X level in the organization?

How much direct access will I have to the senior management of the organization?

What type of contribution does the organization make to the local community?

What type of social activities does the company organize for its employees?

Is a car provided for travelling? Do they pay for gas for travelling done for work purposes?

How would you describe the company's culture and management style?

What are your expectations of new hires?

What is the turnover rate for this position?

What are the company's plans for future growth?

What type of computer skills are necessary for this position?

What role does the Human Resources Department play in the organization?

How has the company handled the recent recession?

Let your roommates know you may be expecting very important calls.

Shelly Broad
Financial Forecast Analyst,
Union Gas Ltd.,
Wilfrid Laurier University Grad '94

The Interview

7

Overall Strategy

Recruiters all recognize that hiring university graduates is like trying to predict the weather, or dabble in futures, in other words, a very risky business. Risky yet essential, because they all know that the person they hire today could well be tomorrow's operations manager, executive director, chief engineer, vice president or sales manager. As a result, the correct assessment and evaluation of you and your graduating class as potential employees (mostly people with almost no track record or history) is one of the business world's toughest challenges.

Remember throughout the process that you are being hired for your potential ability. Their objective is to assess not only your ability but your manageability. Manageability is that relatively rare ability among new graduates to accept criticism and guidance and display a willingness to accept direction. Other determining factors will include your problem solving acumen, your verbal and written skills, your listening ability as well as initiative and energy. In the end, their hiring decisions will be judgement calls. They are all betting on the future with scant information about the past.

The most important strategy when approaching the interview is to think about what the evaluators are looking for, keeping in mind that at the end of each interview most complete an evaluation form. While each organization's evaluation form is different, the basic evaluation criteria remain the same. I will first review interview formats and then those key criteria. I'll then examine what interviewers are looking for and what they may ask in order to achieve their hiring objectives. Then I'll review the approach you should take when answering the questions.

What really turns me off a candidate is attitude. If they don't know anything at all about our company, are they really interested in us?

Jennifer Gay
Coordinator, Staffing and
Organizational Development,
MPR Teltech Ltd.

Interview Formats

Single interview hiring

Although rare, there are still some organizations who will make their hiring decisions based on just one interview. You may even get a verbal offer at the end of the interview. It is obviously at the company's discretion whether or not to do it this way, but it can cause you some difficulty. Because of the speed of the process and, often the need to make a decision quickly, be sure you get all the facts. Try to convey the importance of the decision you have to make to the organization. You must also be able to measure the position along with others you are considering, using the same yardstick.

A series of interviews

These will generally begin with a first screening interview, either on campus or at the organization. In many circumstances, the initial screening interview is conducted by a human resources manager alone or with a line manager. Although not customary, but certainly becoming more common, a telephone screening or video conferencing interview can occur. This method is used mainly by companies located in isolated areas where face-to-face meetings with every qualified candidate is simply impossible.

Subsequent interviews are more intensive than screening interviews. As you progress through the series, you will often be interviewed by people with increasing levels of decision-making authority. A company tour and/or breakfast, lunch or dinner are often included as part of the process.

The following formats are conventionally used in carrying out both single and a series of interviews:

One-on-one/Two-on-one

Your conduct in both types of interviews should be the same. Do not be intimidated by the two-on-one interviews. Contrary to popular belief, they are generally no more difficult than one-on-one interviews. Just remember the importance of paying equal attention to both interviewers. The best way is to talk primarily to the person who asked you the specific question, occasionally turning your head to look at the second interviewer. Be sure you never use the strategy that some interviewees have chosen. They assess who is the more senior interviewer and then proceed to address all answers and their attention only to that person. Don't. You will alienate the second interviewer, who may then surely persuade the other interviewer or the selection committee that you are not worth further interest because you already displayed a tendency to play politics.

Panel interviews

These are not common for entry level positions but if you are unfortunate enough to face one, they can be very intimidating. This is generally because of the size of the room and the number of people present, rather than the interview itself. Just stay focussed and answer the questions the same way. Remember to pay attention to all the interviewers throughout the process.

General Guidelines

1. Remember that by the end of each interview, interviewer/s must make a "yes" or "no" decision. By the time you leave the interview, you must have presented your entire case. There is no second chance to impress them if you are not given a second opportunity. This is equally true whether it is a hiring decision or a "pass on to the next stage" decision.

2. Remember the importance of maintaining eye contact. If you don't, the interviewers will often interpret it as insecurity, a lack of self confidence or that you are not comfortable with the questions or answers. If you look away when asked a question, an interviewer will often dig deeper, believing they are onto something particularly revealing about your personality.

3. Reviewers know that interviewees have learned answers or will respond with what they think the recruiter wants to hear. To overcome this, the seasoned recruiter will wait patiently after an answer because your response will often be followed by what one might call a "qualifier" which can reveal your true feelings or beliefs.

    A typical scenario may be as follows:

    Question: Do you enjoy working in teams or do you prefer working alone? (Your research has told you that all the work at the organization is done in a team environment.)

Do not wish to be anything but what you are, and try to be that perfectly.

St. Francis de Sales

Have fun, find out if this is the type of place you want to work.

Dawn Ursuliak
Risk Management Analyst,
TransAlta Utilities Corporation
University of Alberta Grad '93

You respond: "I really prefer working in teams… (no response from the interviewer)… most of the time", you add.

They will listen carefully to each word of your response to ensure they do not miss those crucial qualifiers, which will be a signal for them to probe much further. They will ask for details, reasons why things were done, or were not done, and so on. Be sure that when you review your practice sessions, you listen carefully for this and make the necessary adjustments to your answering style.

4. Do not be shy to take notes. You cannot be expected to remember every detail after the interview. Take notes judiciously, however, and record only the most important information. You don't want to lose eye contact with the interviewer/s or for the flow of the interview to be broken because of your note taking.

Composure

The assessment will begin from the moment they first meet you and it will continue throughout the process during office visits, second interviews, meals and cocktail parties. No matter what they tell you, they will never stop assessing you, so don't fall for the line "we can all relax now and enjoy ourselves…". But more about that later. In many high pressure industries, they will have a mechanism to evaluate your performance under pressure. While the American recruiters have gained a reputation for using these tactics more often than their Canadian counterparts, you should be prepared for this approach particularly if your research tells you to expect it.

Recruiters will be on the lookout for signs that you do not react well under pressure. In many cases, they will ask you unusual or unexpected questions to gauge your reaction. They aren't looking for a specific answer but rather your reaction to the unexpected. They'll be watching your facial expressions, following your gaze, looking for chair-tilting, any signs of jumpiness, nail-biting, slouching or constant switching of positions in your chair.

"Unexpected" questions

If you could return to any age in history, where would you go?

If you could have dinner with anyone in the world tonight, who would it be? Why? Where?

If you were sent alone to a fully equipped, safe, luxurious island in the Caribbean and could only take three books to read, which would you take?

If you were suddenly made dean of your faculty, what one change would you make immediately?

There really is no preparation you can do for this type of question. Hopefully, your research will have indicated whether they are likely to crop up or not. Think of how you would answer the above questions and the thought process you would follow. My one piece of advice is if you need to buy time, repeat the question slowly and even ask for a clarification if necessary. It is amazing what you can come up with in a very short period of time.

"Technical" questions

What do you think of the packaging on our product X? (Often the product is then shown to you)

Do you think it was a wise move for our company to open a division in Mexico?

Many people regard this type of question as a test of your real interest in the position and the company, and the amount of research you have done. It will also test your composure and ability to think on your feet. Always be prepared for this type of question.

"It appears to be technical" questions

These questions do not test your technical knowledge but rather your ability to think on your feet and logically solve problems. While you can never be prepared for all of them, you can practice answering questions like them. The problem is that recruiters will use a wide variety of questions to ensure you haven't rehearsed any answers. The best advice I can give you is that you remain calm and try to be as logical as possible.

When I recently asked a student how she would find out the number of gas stations in Canada, she told me that she would get copies of all the phone books in the country, go through them, and count the number of the gas stations. Would this work? Possibly… but it is undoubtedly not the most effective or time efficient method. Are recruiters looking for the right answer? They probably don't even know the answer themselves. They are assessing your ability to remain calm and be logical and sensible in your approach. Again, if you want to buy time, ask questions like "how long do I have to answer the question?" and "what resources do I have at my disposal?".

"Hypothetical" Questions

Interviewers will present you with a hypothetical problem or situation and ask you how you would react. My advice is that you pause and take time to answer the question. You want to immediately show the interviewer that you are giving the answer careful thought. If you need further clarification, ask for it. It will give you a little more time to think and will provide you with some of the interviewer's thoughts on the situation. They are generally not looking for a detailed solution but rather, they are assessing your analytical ability and your problem solving skills.

You should try to cover each of the following steps in your analysis:

Collect all the relevant information and data

Ask questions

Validate information received

Seek expert advice, if necessary and available

Consider all the alternative solutions

Make a decision

Communicate the decision

Monitor the result of the decision

Later in the chapter, you'll find a comprehensive list of typical questions that are asked in interviews and a strategy for answering the toughest ones.

Communication of Ideas

Throughout the process, they will be assessing your ability to express your ideas, thoughts and feelings clearly. The weight given to the assessment of this criterion will depend entirely on the type of position for which you are applying. They will not be assessing your language skills but rather your ability to express ideas in a clear and logical manner. The key to doing well in this area is to be very well prepared. You will discover, as you go through the process, that your ability to express yourself clearly improves with each and every interview. Practice is the key. The best way to do this is to rehearse answering questions with friends and family. Don't learn your answers by heart. Practice answering questions and you will be amazed how quickly and easily, even in these informal settings, your thoughts will start to make more sense and your answers begin to flow. Like a musician or athlete, the more you practise, the more natural all the movements begin to feel. If you can record your practice sessions and then review them, they will be even more effective.

One of the most crucial mistakes people make is to listen to the first half of a question and rather than wait for the rest, they jump in. This makes a very poor impression. A recruiter will envision you doing this in a business setting to your clients or customers. It can also lead to uncomfortable moments as the interviewer tries to end the question and you try to backtrack graciously. Another common mistake is to constantly use pat phrases and slang expressions. If you have recorded one of your practice sessions, listen carefully for the use of these and others:

"…OK"	"Wanna…"
"To tell you the truth…"	"Kinda…"
"Frankly…"	"Like, you know…"
"Basically…"	"Yeah…"
"You know…"	"'Cause…"

Used over and over again, they will be distracting to you and certainly to an interviewer. Avoid them at all costs.

In a behavioural-interviewing setting, if you have never experienced what they are asking, answer by saying "what you would have done in that situation?"

Rachelle Kowal
Business Analyst, TransAlta
Utilities Corporation, University
of Saskatchewan Grad '95

Self Confidence

There is a fine line between arrogant and self assured, cocky and confident. What the recruiters are attempting to do throughout the entire process is to uncover your real personality. This is often best judged not in the interview scenario, but at cocktail parties, lunches, career fairs or other sources to which the recruiters have access. Another evaluating technique will be to ask you about your past "great" accomplishments and "poor" performances. The arrogant person usually blames others for his/her failures, and takes credit for "everyone's" achievements. Asking tough questions or continually asking "why", will often bring out the worst in the arrogant candidate, so beware. If they are having doubts, they may try being critical of something you have done or decisions you have made.

Other "uncovering" questions:

> How do you rank among your peers?
> Why did you choose your university?
> What do you think you have learned at school (other than technical) that will help you in your job?
> Which of your personal traits are you most/least proud of?
> What is there about yourself that you would like most to change?

Motivation and Ambition

Recruiters are going to want to know as much about your motivations, your future plans and goals as possible. They are going to assess your interest in their field or industry and your knowledge of the job. They will measure your real interest in working for the particular company or organization. Research and preparation are again the key.

Personal motivation-related questions they may ask are:

> What has been your greatest accomplishment in a work environment and why?
> What motivates you?
> If you were them, why would you hire you?
> What kinds of things would you want to avoid in future jobs?

Give us an example from your past that demonstrates your perseverance.

Tell us about a project that really got you motivated and enthused.

How do you feel about your academic achievement?

What types of tasks or projects do you find most/least challenging?

Work Experience

Most interviewers will question and assess the validity, relevance and value of your past work experience. They know that many people tend to "exaggerate" the importance of their employment experience. For example, saying they were an assistant manager when they were a sales clerk, or implying they were a bookkeeper when in fact they were a filing clerk. They will check into your past jobs, not only superficially, but in depth to discover if what you wrote on your CACEE form or resume is true.

Other typical questions regarding your work experience are:

Question: What exactly did you do as a sales clerk?
Response: Don't only tell what you did, but what you learned and how it is relevant to the job for which you are interviewing.

Question: To whom did you report?
Response: Explain who the person was, what their role was in the company and how the reporting structure worked.

Question: What did you sell? How did you sell the product? (if applicable) What was your sales volume?
Response: If you were selling a product or service, make sure you have all the facts and figures at hand. Nothing is more disconcerting than a candidate who cannot remember any details about the product with which they were so closely associated. How many "widgets" did you sell? What was the selling price? What was the marketing strategy? and other product related questions.

Question: What did you do on a typical day at work?
Response: Take a "typical" day that shows responsibility, achievement and the fact that you were busy. Only you'll know how typical the day you describe really was.

Research what attitudes the company is looking for as opposed to 'skills'. Obviously the company realizes you can be taught any skill. It is the attitude/character that can not be taught or changed very easily.

Rachelle Kowal
Business Analyst, TransAlta
Utilities Corporation, University
of Saskatchewan Grad '95

Question: Why did you/didn't you return the following summer (to a job)?

Response: If you have worked at the same organization for many summers, they may ask you why you did not look for fresh challenges. In the case of continued employment with one organization, be able to show that you have had additional responsibility or learned new skills. Conversely, if you changed jobs every summer, they may well ask you why you never returned to a job. Be prepared to show that you wanted to learn new skills and needed new challenges that were not possible in that position.

Attitude

Your attitude will be assessed every step of the way. There are a few specific questions which will help recruiters assess it in an interview setting:

> Asking questions about courses in which you obtained your lowest grades
>
> Asking about your least favourite course/professor or job

Questions such as:

> Have you ever been in a dispute with a supervisor? What was it about and how was it resolved?
>
> Have you ever been in a dispute with a co-worker? What was it about and how was it resolved?
>
> Tell us about a time when you came up with a new method or suggestion that was rejected?
>
> We would be interested to hear about an occasion when your work or performance was criticized.
>
> How do you deal with a group or team member who is not doing their part in a project?
>
> Why are you not involved in sports/extracurricular activities/university life (where applicable)?
>
> What was the most difficult decision you have ever had to make?

As each situation arises, try not to blame others for your problems or failures. Find the positive aspects of each, stressing what you learned and how it will enable you to cope with sticky situations that may arise in future jobs.

Energy level

This will be ascertained not through questions but your energy from your resume or CACEE form, which will give them insight into the kind of life you lead. Many interviewers will ask you to describe a typical day, week or weekend in your life. Make sure the one you describe is filled with energy and activity. Throughout the interview process, you will be constantly observed, so your physical and mental energy levels should be high. But do not burn the midnight oil the night before a major recruiting event. Plan your schedule to allow yourself sufficient recovery time.

Language skills

The ability to speak languages other than your mother tongue is regarded by almost every recruiter as a major plus, whether or not it's a requirement of the job, so it's essential that you clearly indicate your knowledge of other languages on your resume. In addition, it is important that you state your proficiency for each "other" language. If it is a requirement of the job, your language skills will be tested orally. If the position calls for advanced writing skills, don't be surprised if you are tested in some way as well. If you have stated that you speak both French and English fluently, you can expect to have at least part of one interview in the second language. If you have stated that you speak some "other language" fluently, it is unlikely that you will be asked to speak it. You never know, however, when you will meet someone who just happens to speak the language. Will it cost you the job if you don't speak "other" languages as well as you stated? Possibly but it will in all likelihood leave you flustered and uncomfortable and certainly not capable of performing at your peak for the rest of the interview.

Academic performance

Your academic performance will have been one of the major factors in the selection process for the interview. Interviewers will still undoubtedly want to discuss it at some length during the interview itself. For those of you who are in the top ten percent of your class, your task is easy. Be prepared to be complimented on your achievements and to be asked why and how you did so well. I strongly suggest that you stick to all the positive aspects of your performance. Your discipline in keeping up to date with each class, your excellent organization skills, your ability to take comprehensive notes and your genuine interest in your courses and program.

Steer far away from ever putting down your fellow students. I recently asked a top "academic achievement" student a question and I was told "I am extremely bright, I have an IQ of 148, and most of the students in my classes aren't very smart". Another interviewee told me "unlike most students in my class, I don't skip classes and I never do my assignments at the last minute".

Remember, no matter how terrific your grades are, recruiters are wary about hiring people with a bad attitude. They are disruptive and very difficult to manage. Worst of all, they reflect badly on the hirer.

For those of you in the other ninety percent of the class, wherever possible, try to stress things like improved performance and better grades in your specialty areas. Try to show a link between your academic performance and your other activities and involvement; the time spent working at doing part-time jobs, community, or on-campus extracurricular activities can go a long way towards depicting you as a multi-faceted person, so stress this.

Be sure you can explain the reason for any courses in which you have performed exceptionally poorly. Do not blame the lecturer, your examination schedule, course text books or material. It will be interpreted very negatively and the interviewer will undoubtedly envisage you on the job, blaming your supervisor or colleagues for any thing that goes wrong. They will often question courses in progress, dropped, missed, deferred or failed, so be prepared to explain each with sound reasons.

Leadership

This is a difficult area because most organizations are looking for people who will ultimately be able to lead, but who will initially be able to follow. They hope to hire someone who will, in the short term, be willing to do routine, often mundane work but in the medium to long term, will be able to take on responsibility and do complex tasks.

What makes your job more difficult is proving to a recruiter that you will be the perfect candidate to fulfil both these seemingly contrary objectives. The best way to do this is to show that you have held leadership positions or supervisory positions that required problem solving and decision making.

Don't try to fake this because recruiters know that candidates all want to show that they have been the boss, the manager, crew chief, the assistant manager, the captain or the president. They will dig deep to ascertain your honesty and to find out how valid the leadership positions are. Did you have real responsibility and authority? Did you really have to lead people?

In a recent interview the candidate, who had been working at a retail store for the past two summers, had stated that she was the assistant manager. When I asked why she thought they promoted her to this position and what additional responsibilities it encompassed, she embarrassingly said they had never really told her she was the assistant manager but that on two occasions, in the previous eighteen months, the manager had left the store early and asked her to lock-up. She assumed this meant she was "like" an assistant manager.

The following are questions you may be asked:

Tell me about a situation where you had to put a team together successfully.

How did you motivate a group you had to lead?

Describe the best manager you ever had.

Describe the qualities of the worst manager you ever had and what you would have done in the circumstances.

What did you like about being in charge?

How did your peers act toward you when you were in charge? How did you feel?

Can you tell us about a time you led a group of people to do something?

With respect to manageability, they will ask you in depth questions about how you were previously supervised, how closely your performance has been monitored in previous positions and how you felt about doing mundane, repetitive or boring tasks:

Have you ever had to do tasks you regarded as boring?

What were your feelings and reactions to these tasks?

Did you get bored easily?

How do you react to criticism?

Describe the worst position you've ever had.

For bigger companies, the first interview is often someone from Human Resources. Therefore, emphasize the points that an HR person can relate to... don't degenerate into technical mumbo-jumbo; explain your work in terms that your parents could understand.

Gerald Boersma
Software Engineer,
MPR Teltech Ltd.,
Carlton University Grad '95

Slow the talking down...take the time to digest the questions before answering.

Melissa Monk
Intermediate Auditor,
Richter, Usher & Vineberg,
Concordia University Grad '94

Learn from the mistakes or practice with someone before you go into an interview.

Paul Raj
Mine Planning Engineer,
Syncrude Canada Ltd.,
University of Alberta Grad '95

Team player

Your research should give you insight into how important this quality is for each position for which you apply. My advice is simple but extremely important. Do yourself and the organization interviewing you a favour. Be honest. If, for example, you know the position requires you to work alone for days, weeks, or even months on end and you really are uncomfortable with the prospect, do not say you love working alone just to try to get the job. Undoubtedly, after a very short time, you are going to be miserable.

Conversely, if you love working alone and everything in the organization happens in teams, pretending to be a good team player and getting the position is only going to make you unhappy after a short time on the job.

If faced with such a situation, you must ask yourself if it is worth going to an interview when you know you are going to be really unhappy with the position.

Let us assume that you are a perfect fit for the position. If it involves team work, they are expecting you to say "I like to work on teams, I want to work on teams, I work well with teams, I lead teams, I find that I perform at my peak in a team environment". Or with respect to working alone "I love working alone, I work best when I am alone, I thrive when I work alone". Their objective is to find out the truth. They will ask you a series of questions designed to find out what you are really like. Your answers will be challenged. The best proof is to give examples in each case to support your answers before they have to question your response.

Typical questions you may be asked:

> When you are assigned to work with new people or on a team at school, how do you go about getting to know them and how they work?
> Do you prefer working alone or with others? Why?
> What type of person is the hardest for you to get along with?
> Tell us about your experience in working on teams/working alone.
> What is your usual contribution to a team?
> What do you get out of working on a team?
> What kind of people annoy you the most?

Concentrate on showing the interviewer that you can do the job.

Debbie Ng
Software Designer,
Unisys GSG Canada Inc.,
McGill University Grad '94

Extremely pushy, persistent students really turn me off.

Noni Wright
Recruitment & Selection
Coordinator,
TransAlta Utilities Corporation

Where positions require you to spend time working in both situations described above, give examples from your past where you have had the opportunity to work in both types of environments and why you have and will continue to excel at both.

The ability to think on one's feet

This is certainly a key factor for success in many fields. Some interviewers think this approach is too harsh for the first job seekers. However, if you are applying for a high stress position or one where the need to be quick on one's feet is a key component of the job, expect to be tested in some way or another. What they are trying to assess is how you will deal with unexpected situations. Will you panic when a client, customer or manager asks you a tough question for which you are not prepared? How will you respond? If it appears to the interviewer that you were prepared for the question he or she asked, they will continue to ask you further questions until they will feel they have caught you off-guard. The purpose is not to trick you or to see you squirm; it is to see how well you react after the initial surprise. Some may feel they tested your reactions sufficiently when assessing your composure; others may want to assess it separately.

Anticipate questions related to the job and based on your experience as it applies to the job.

Sue Riddell
Manager, Employment & Staffing,
DuPont Canada Inc.

Some possible questions they may ask:

> Which Canadian business person do you admire the most and why?
> How do you define success?
> If you are forced to spend 24 hours on a plane sitting next to anyone in the world – not family, or girlfriend/boyfriend, who would you choose?
> What person would you say has had the most significant influence on your life? Why?

Try to buy a little thinking time, think logically and remember that there are generally no right or wrong answers to this type of question.

Manageability

The opening paragraph to this chapter described manageability as that intangible quality within you that is going to enable an organization to successfully manage, train and develop your career, both short and long term. Borrowing three phrases from well-known commercials, it is how successful they will be at "Bringing out the best in you" and "Allowing you to be all that you can be" without having "To do it all for you".

Your manageability will generally be assessed in two ways. An in-depth analysis of your work history will be done. Your reaction to instruction, to close supervision, to evaluation and to criticism will also be assessed. This will be done by asking about your reaction to each of the aforementioned points with reference to your previous jobs. You will be asked to give your perception of the roles of managers, supervisors, performance evaluations and the importance of training.

Typical questions that may be asked:

> What qualities should a successful manager possess?
> How have past managers encouraged your best performance?
> How do you react to criticism?
> Why do you think performance evaluations are important?
> Do you think formal staff training courses are valuable?
> What benefit do you think you will gain from our staff training program?

Decision-making ability

Most students truly believe they've made very few decisions in their lives and are uncomfortable when asked questions about their decision making ability. Few major decisions perhaps, but everyone makes decisions every day, so bear this in mind. They will simply be assessing your thought processes, your research talents and decision-making ability.

These questions could be asked:

> How and why did you choose your high school, college and university?
> How and why did you choose your degree?
> Why a double major, or minor in X?
> Why did you choose to travel Europe last summer and not work?
> How did you go about choosing your electives?
> Why did you choose to apply to the particular organization?
> Did you simply follow your friends? Did your parents tell you what to do?

They need to assess if you are going to be able to make sound, important decisions once you are on the job. Prove to them that you will.

General Probing Questions

These questions are typical of the general probing type of questions designed to uncover relevant information from you.

1. Asking you to compare two events, jobs, or people in your life:
    eg. How would you compare your job at Eaton vs. your job at Camp White River?

2. An interviewer might praise you for something you have accomplished, in an effort to encourage you to offer more information on the subject.
    eg. After just four months as a member of the Marketing Club you became president. That's a terrific accomplishment. How did this happen?

3. You might be asked for specific examples to support how you describe yourself or to elaborate on broad general statements you make during the interview.
    Candidate: I have always enjoyed working with people.
    Interviewer: Please give us examples of what you enjoy about working with people and what you have learned from these experiences.

4. Asking situational questions is a behaviour-based technique whereby a "real" problem is described and you are asked what you did do or would do in the situation.

    Example 1
    If you were a junior auditor and you were left alone at a client for a short period and the owner approached you and asked you what the net profit for the year looked like...

    Example 2
    You are a recently hired consulting engineer and have been asked to attend a meeting, with a supervisor, at a customer site. On arrival, you receive a message that the supervisor's car broke down on the highway and he will be at least two hours late. Your customer is ready to start the meeting.

5. Self-Disclosure is a technique by which the interviewer discloses something of a personal nature, true or fictional, to help you feel comfortable and relaxed about revealing potentially sensitive information.

121

Example 1

I also had a problem with a few courses at school, particularly in my second year. How did you feel your second year went? (Particularly effective for a sudden lowering of marks.)

Example 2

"I sometimes get really frustrated working in teams. I often end up forgetting about everyone else and do things on my own". Their technique, where they believe they may have uncovered a potential weakness, is to create a scenario whereby they empathise with your possible problem, trying to get you to reveal something you otherwise would not have said.

Illegal and Improper Questions

The question I get asked most frequently following presentations on interview techniques is how to deal appropriately with illegal or improper questions. My advice is always the same: think carefully about why you are being asked the question.

Is it relevant to the job and is it just an indication of the recruiter's beliefs and feelings or those of the organization as a whole?

One of the best answers I've heard to this type of question was related by a student a few years ago. She was asked by an interviewer, a senior manager with the organization, if she intended to have children in the near future. She responded by saying that she would answer the questions if the interviewer would tell her why it was an important criterion for the position. He looked embarrassed and said that it was not, but that he was just curious. If that was the case, she said, she did not feel it was necessary to answer an irrelevant question. No, she did not get the job. But she quite rightly observed that she had no interest in working for someone for whom her personal life was a curiosity.

Some questions that should not be asked:

> What nationality are you?
> Is your last name (ethnic origin)?
> What church are you a member of?

Do you belong to the X church or synagogue?

What does your spouse/girlfriend/boyfriend (mother or father) do for a living?

Are you planning any additions to your family?

Do you speak, read or write a foreign language? (If it was not stated on your CACEE form or resume)

What was your mother's maiden name?

Was your name ever changed from what it is now?

Do you have a bank account? (Checking account, stocks, bonds, own your own home, own rental property...)

Is your roommate male or female?

Any questions relating to your political feelings.

There are many more "illegal" questions. In general, you should never be asked anything related to age, sex, colour, race, creed, national origin, religious persuasion, marital status, political beliefs, physical well-being or disabilities.

If you are ever faced with these types of questions in an interview, speak to someone at your Career Centre immediately. For a province by province reference, the Canadian Human Rights Commission chart *Employment: Prohibited grounds of discrimination* appears in Appendix III at the end of this book.

Be yourself – the rest will come naturally. You do not want to be hired based on what an organization 'expects' you to be – you want to be hired based on who you are and what you have to offer.

Alex Gallacher
Manager, Human Resources,
Mintz & Partners

135 Questions Asked by Interviewers

1. Why did you choose to apply to our organization?
2. What can you offer us?
3. Where do you see yourself in five years? Ten years?
4. Do you plan to return to school for further education?
5. What related skills have you developed?
6. What type of work interests you the most?
7. What did you enjoy most about your last job?
8. What did you least enjoy about your last job?
9. How many levels of management did you interact with at your last job?
10. Can you tell us about a time you led a group of people?

11. Why did you choose your major?
12. What do you consider to be your greatest strengths?
13. Please tell us about your biggest weakness.
14. Would you be successful working on a team?
15. Of which three accomplishments are you most proud?
16. What was the biggest challenge in your last job?
17. Have you ever dropped a course? Why?
18. Why did you select your college or university?
19. Why a double major/minor in X?
20. Which courses did you like the best? Why?
21. Which courses did you like the least? Why?
22. How did you go about choosing your electives?
23. Do you think you received a good education at X?
24. What is your overall average/GPA? What is your major average/GPA?
25. Do you feel that your grades accurately reflect your ability?
26. Were you financially responsible for any portion of your education?
27. Have you worked under deadline pressure? When?
28. How effective have you been in these situations?
29. Are you able to work on several assignments at once?
30. How do you feel about working in a structured environment?
31. How do you feel about working in an unstructured environment?
32. How do you think you will feel about working overtime?
33. How do you think you will feel about working on weekends?
34. Do you have any hobbies?
35. Why are you not involved in sports or extracurricular activities?
36. Are you willing to work flex-time?
37. Have you ever done any volunteer work? What made you get involved?
38. Define success/failure.
39. Have you ever had any failures? How did you feel at the time?
40. How does your education or work experience relate to this job?
41. How did you get along with your former supervisors and co-workers?
42. How many classes did you miss during the course of a semester?
43. What are your salary expectations?
44. Tell me about yourself.

Be yourself. If they don't like you for who you are, then the employer is probably not a good fit for you.

Noreen Teo
Internal Auditor, Union Gas Ltd.,
McMaster University Grad '94

124

45. Do you have any computer experience?

46. Have you ever made a presentation to a group of people? How large a group? How did you feel about doing this?

47. What have you done that demonstrates initiative and willingness to work?

48. Have you ever had to work with a manager who was unfair to you, or who was just plain hard to talk to? Tell me about it.

49. Give me an example of a time when people were really counting on you.

50. How do you handle boring or monotonous tasks?

51. What do you think of the packaging of our product X?

52. Describe your typical weekday/weekend.

53. Have you ever been in a dispute with a co-worker? How was it resolved?

54. What special characteristics should I consider about you?

55. Why did your grades slip during your second semester (or third, fourth)

56. How do you plan your day? Your week?

57. How do you determine your priorities?

58. What happens when two priorities compete for your time?

59. What's the toughest communication problem you have ever faced?

60. Tell me about a time when someone has lost his/her temper with you in a business situation.

61. Have you ever worked in a place where it seemed to be just one crisis after another? If so, tell me about it. (How did you handle it? How did you feel?… etc.)

62. What do you see as some of your most pressing developmental needs?

63. Define cooperation.

64. Describe the best manager you've ever had.

65. Describe the toughest manager you've ever had.

66. For what have you been most frequently criticized?

67. What do you think should determine a person's progress in an organization?

68. What parts of the job do you think you would find most satisfying? Least satisfying?

69. How is your academic/work experience/extracurricular activities relevant to this job?

70. What did you do on a typical day at work?

Be yourself and do not be intimidated by the interviewer.

Lilian Zia
Software Designer,
CAE Electronics Ltd.,
McGill University Grad '94

71. If you were suddenly made dean of your faculty, what one change would you make immediately?

72. What job in our company do you want to work toward?

73. What do you do when you are put in a situation that seems impossible to handle?

74. Have you had the opportunity to work in a group at school?

75. What role do you typically play in the group?

76. What would you do if you were working on a group assignment and someone was clearly not doing his/her share of the work?

77. What do you get out of working on a team?

78. Other than technical material, what do you think you have learned in school that will help you in your job?

79. Which of your personal traits are you most/least proud of?

80. What motivates you to put forth your greatest effort?

81. Are you typically a more dominant or passive member in a group?

82. Tell us about a project that really got you motivated and enthused.

83. Why did/didn't you return the following summer to your job?

84. How would your best friend/enemy describe you?

85. Tell us about a time when you came up with a new method or suggestion that was rejected.

86. Tell us about an occasion when your work or performance was criticized.

87. What complex problems have you solved in your previous positions?

88. Do you set goals for yourself? How do you reach them?

89. What did you like about being in charge?

90. How did your peers act toward you when you were in charge?

91. Have you ever quit a job? Why?

92. Do you get bored easily?

93. How do you respond to criticism?

94. When you are assigned to work with new people or on a team at school, how do you go about getting to know them and how they work?

95. What type of person is the hardest for you to get along with?

96. Give us an example from your past that demonstrates persistence.

97. If you were forced to spend 24 hours on a plane sitting next to anyone in the world – not family, or girlfriend/boyfriend, who would you choose?

98. How have past managers encouraged your best performance?

Rehearse your responses to 'the top 100 questions interviewers ask'. Know why you've applied to the job and why they should hire you above all others.

Dana Tonus
Director, Co-operative Education
& Student Placement,
University of Windsor

I had an interview in which the interviewer did all the talking.

Debbie Ng
Software Designer,
Unisys GSG Canada Inc.,
McGill University Grad '94

99. Why are performance evaluations important?
100. What benefit do you think you will gain from our staff training program?
101. What do you know about our products or services?
102. Why did you choose to travel to Europe last summer and not work?
103. How would you compare your job at X vs. your job at Y?
104. Give me an example of something you've had to give up in order to get a job done?
105. To date, what has impressed you most about our company?
106. Do you prefer large or small organizations? Why?

Uncommon questions and advice on how to answer them effectively

Interviewers will each have their own motivations for asking these questions. My objective is not to analyse why the questions are asked but to advise you on an approach to answering them.

107. *Tell me a joke.*

Keep one handy, not dirty and tellable in mixed company. Although not widely used, quite a few students did tell me how extremely difficult it is to think of a joke on the spot, so you should have one prepared. Keep it short, simple and inoffensive. No sex, religion, race or politics.

108. *Teach me something.*

This is an increasingly more popular question that tests a number of different skills and that can be very tough if you haven't thought about it. Keep it simple and technical but not too technical that you have a problem explaining it in a pressure interview setting. You may want to try a Martial Art, an unusual sport, a musical instrument or perhaps how to use your digital diary, which you just happen to have handy.

109. *If you could go anywhere for a dream weekend, where would it be?*

It is alright to go away and relax with a friend. So many people believe that the answer to this type of question must be work related. Far too many believe the interviewer wants to hear how dedicated they are, so their dream weekend is spent studying or doing research, or attending a technical conference. No one is going to believe that, so use the opportunity to show how well rounded you are and that you enjoy life beyond work.

In a third interview for a company the VP interviewed me and asked strange questions. "Would you mow the lawn if I asked you?" and "Would you work for free?" These aren't your typical interview questions. I'm not sure what impression I left, but he left a bad impression on me. Needless to say, I am not working there.

Kelly Collver
Marketing Assistant,
DuPont Canada Inc.,
McMaster University Grad '94

The first question I was asked in an interview was if I could play goalie for their hockey team!

Jason Toledano
Staff Accountant,
Mintz & Partners,
York University Grad '94

110. *What is your favourite movie?*

The choice is yours, but be prepared to give details and the reasons why the movie is your favourite. I recently had an interviewee immediately name his favourite movie with confidence, but when asked he couldn't name one actor in the movie or even give a brief description of the plot.

111. *How would you go about ascertaining how many bridges, gas stations, traffic lights or children under 13 there are in Canada?*

This is a question that seems to throw most people into a tailspin because they believe the interviewer is looking for an exact answer. For all questions of this type, the interviewer is looking for deductive logic and your ability to think clearly under pressure. Keep your cool and think before your speak. Go slowly and don't say anything outrageous. Tell them each of your assumptions and they should be satisfied.

112. *If you were being sent to a fully equipped, safe, but deserted island for a week, what three books would you take with you to read?*

I've asked this question a few thousand times and have heard some really unusual answers. It is, once again, your opportunity to show the breadth of your personality and the fact that your interests are multi-faceted. Forget your school books. The interviewer will question your sincerity. The worst response I ever had to this question was a student who told me he would take his Finance textbooks because he was about three weeks behind in his course work. I know that if I had asked him if he regularly kept up to date with his assignments, he would have answered yes.

113. *If you could have dinner tomorrow night with anyone in the world, who would it be?*

Again, your opportunity to show the breadth of your interests and your personality. Forget the sport heroes and the soap opera stars and display some depth. Be prepared to explain why and relate one question you'd want to ask your guest.

114. *Why should we hire you rather than another candidate?*

115. *We only hire the best. Do you fall into this category?*

116. *Are you better than most people in your class?*

Prepare, prepare, prepare.

Bruce Walker
Coordinator, Recruitment,
Union Gas Ltd.

117. *Why would you hire "you" for this position?*

Many people are intimidated by these questions. Don't be. You should expect at least one question like this, so be prepared. This is a really great question for you because it gives you an ideal opportunity to quote from your "best qualities card" directly without having to fit it awkwardly into another answer. Be positive, say that it is impossible for you to know the qualifications of the other candidates, but that you can tell them why you would be perfect for the job. Even if you know some of the other candidates, don't discuss them. Putting other people down is never a good strategy. Focus on your achievements.

118. *Do you prefer working in a team or working on your own?*

119. *Would you describe yourself as more analytical or verbal?*

The "right" answer to this type of question is totally dependant on the specific requirements of the position. My advice is rather than concern yourself with the correct answer, reply honestly to the questions. If they are really looking for a person who only wants to work alone and is not verbal, and this does not apply to you, it's better to find out at this stage of the process. If you like both working environments, say so. If you believe you are far more analytical or verbal, don't be afraid to say so.

120. *How do you feel about travelling?*

121. *How do you feel about the possibility of relocating?*

Again the truth is the only answer. If it is a major requirement for the position, the only way you'll be happy long term, is if you answer the question honestly. There is no point in saying you don't mind relocating only to find yourself being asked to relocate after six months and being forced to resign because you really don't want to.

122. *What is the hardest decision you have ever had to make?*

Don't tell the interviewer you have never had to make a difficult decision. If you do, you are not answering the question, because they are not asking if you have ever had a hard decision to make. They are asking you, of all the decisions you have made, which has been the most difficult. If you say you have never had to make a difficult decision, you may frighten them off.

Recognize what an interview is and what it isn't. It is not a rehashing of your resume but an opportunity to take the initiative to sell yourself and in order to sell yourself, you need to know yourself.

Jill Curley
Career Placement Counsellor,
Mount Saint Vincent University

They will imagine that if faced with a difficult decision on the job, you would not be able to cope.

123. *If you were hiring for this position, what qualities would be important?*

This is an excellent question to test your knowledge of the position and the quality of the research you have done on the position. Obviously, you would like to repeat your best qualities but be subtle and rephrase them. Show the interviewers you really understand what they are looking for.

124. *Are you interviewing anywhere else?*

Many people, and I am one of them, believe that it is wrong to ask an interviewee this question. How would an interviewer feel if an interviewee asked him or her for a list of other candidates being interviewed for the position? You should be as polite as possible and say yes or no, as the case may be. If you have answered yes and they ask you who else you are interviewing with, I believe you should simply say that you would prefer not to give the names of the companies.

125. *Name a book that's had a big influence on your life.*

Be prepared for this popular question. Make sure you can tell the interviewers details about the book, what specific influence it has had on your life and why.

126. *Who has been your role model?*

127. *Who is your biggest hero? Why?*

128. *Which Canadian business person do admire the most? Why?*

129. *What person has had the most influence on you life? Why?*

Think of someone from any walk of life who has achieved something meaningful and try to avoid your sports heros. Be prepared to discuss the person and their life in some detail in case you happen to pick a person the interviewers know a lot about. A parent is a possible and popular answer. Make sure you can explain why, other than the fact that they have raised you.

130. *If you could return to any age in history, where would you go? Why?*

A favourite of interviewers who like to test your creativity and the depth of your personality.

Think about this question before you are interviewed because it tends to leave some interviewees speechless or it solicits superficial answers from the unprepared.

131. *What do you know about our organization?*

This is a tough question because what they are really testing is the quality of the research you have done and what you have learned from the research. Prepare to answer this question. It will be another excellent opportunity to sell yourself and your excellent fit with the organization.

132. *How do you rank among your peers?*

This is very similar to the question about why they should hire you and not another candidate. Your response should also be the same. You don't know the other candidates so don't try to compare yourself. The only tangible method of comparison is your academic standing in class. If you know this, discuss it if you feel it is to your benefit.

133. *Describe your ideal job.*

Most people will question whether there is such a thing as an ideal job. Use it as the perfect opportunity to show your understanding of the position and the skills required to excel at it. You should not, however, repeat the job description, word for word, it will be too obvious.

134. *What do think about the current situation in…?*

A tough question because it means you must be up to date on current events around the world. As you are going to have to be current enough to carry on a social conversation in the other phases of the recruiting process, you may as well start reading the newspaper, watching the evening news and keeping up to date on current events.

135. *If we were to offer you a job today would you accept it?*

If you are interested in the position, say so. This may not be an offer at all, but rather it could be a "set-up" to see how you will react if someone else makes you an offer in this way. Even if you are extremely interested avoid the temptation to immediately respond that you would accept. Explain the importance of your completing the recruiting process and considering all your options. It is perfectly acceptable to say you feel uncomfortable cancelling other second interviews. You will be respected for your professionalism.

Technical questions

Many people believe that the toughest question to deal with is, in fact, the technical question to which you don't know the answer. My advice is to be honest and say that you do not know the answer. If it is something that has not yet been covered in your courses, say so. It is far better than trying to pretend you do and fumbling through an answer. Admit you don't know the answer. If appropriate, explain to the interviewer how you would go about finding the answer. It will have a far less negative impact on the rest of the interview than pretending to know. If it is something that you should have learned through your research, let it be a lesson for future interviews.

Second Interviews

To be consistent, I will refer to all interviews held after the initial interview as second interviews throughout this chapter. If you have your first interview on campus, then chances are you will have your second at the organization's offices. If you have your first interview at the organization, many of the things discussed in this chapter will happen immediately following the first interview.

You will also hear second interviews being referred to as call-backs, site visits, follow-up interviews, final interviews or office interviews. Whatever they are called, the objective is the same. The organization wants an opportunity for a number of different people to meet you and for you to get a feel for the ambiance of the operation in action. You'll have the opportunity to meet people at all levels of the organization and to ask questions you didn't ask in the first interview because you were still learning the ropes.

These interviews take various forms depending on the organization but they will often include some or all of the following common elements:

An in-depth tour of the facility

A series of interviews and meetings with people ranging from senior management to very recent graduates. These may be line managers with whom you may be working, or they may be managers chosen to represent all the line managers and to select staff on their behalf. Some may include a form of technical or aptitude testing. Many will include a meal or cocktail reception as part of the process.

Whatever they include, they should be thought of as an event rather than an interview because few will be restricted to just one interview. They are time consuming and exhausting. You will need to be both physically and mentally prepared to be at your very best for the whole event.

General advice

Do as much research as you can on the organization's second interview process. Students who have gone through the process before are obviously your best source of information. Ask your contact for a detailed schedule of the event. Try to find out exactly what the individual components of the day will be and the time frame. The fewer surprises you have, the better. Generally, you will not be able, nor should you attempt, to schedule two second interviews on the same day. You will be too tired to perform well in the second one, and knowing you have another gruelling test to follow, will probably adversely affect your performance in the first.

Dress requirements are the same as for first interviews, unless you have been told otherwise. Make sure you get all the details concerning the dress expectations well before the interview.

You will usually be given a choice of dates and times for a second interview. Try to fit them into your school schedule as much as possible, but they may mean you'll have to miss classes. This is particularly true for out-of-town interviews. Take the time to explain the situation to your professors. Most of them will be very understanding. While you are in the process of scheduling the appointment with the organization, make sure you let them see that you are flexible. All too often students are totally uncompromising when it comes to availability for second interviews, and they unintentionally give the recruiters the impression that they are not particularly interested in the position. If a date or time is impossible for you, explain the situation and they'll probably offer you an alternative time or date.

The day before the interview, phone and confirm the time, date and location. If you are not familiar with the location, you should also confirm the easiest route there. If you are travelling from out of town, confirm the travel arrangements.

Remembering names and faces

It will make a very good impression if you remember the names and faces of the people you meet. Review the names of the people from the organization you have met before you attend the second interview, try to remember what they look like so that when you meet them you can call them by their name. They will be flattered and impressed.

Your arrival

Arrive at the location about ten to fifteen minutes before the interview's scheduled time. If you're worried about the reliability of public transport, plan to be there forty-five minutes before the interview time. As suggested with first interviews, take a few moments to adjust your appearance and to compose yourself. This can be done in the company's washroom or in a public washroom. You don't want to sit in the reception area for more than five minutes as this is when your anxiety usually reaches its peak. Take along something to read to occupy yourself. Be warm and friendly to everyone you meet, but don't feel the need to pour out your heart to the receptionist. This idle chatter will only increase your nervousness. Instead, try to get a feel for the atmosphere in the organization.

The interviews

Some organizations are very structured in the way they conduct second interviews. Often, each interviewer is given a set of evaluation criteria that must be covered and often a list of questions that must be asked, in order to complete an evaluation form. Sometimes, the structure of the interview is left entirely up to the interviewer. In both cases, the questions asked are pretty much the same as in the first interview, with one possible exception. You are far more likely to be asked technical questions in the second interview,

I'm really turned off by someone who constantly interrupts an interviewer or defensively asks why a question was asked when it is clearly based on a bona fide job related criteria.

Alex Gallacher
Manager, Human Resources,
Mintz & Partners

134

particularly by line managers you'll inevitably meet. Meeting them will also give you the opportunity to ask all the technical questions you have as well.

The interviews will vary greatly in length and intensity. The shortest I've ever heard about was ten minutes, the longest two and a quarter hours. The majority are, thankfully, somewhere in between. Your participation in each type of interview will also vary greatly and will depend on the seniority of the person doing the interview. As a general rule, the more senior the interviewer, the more they tend to speak and consequently, the less you'll be expected to say. Most of the senior people you'll meet will have had very little experience dealing with entry level staff, so they'll probably spend most of the time selling the organization to you. If you find yourself in this type of situation, let the interviewer dictate the pace and flow. Don't feel obliged to talk if it doesn't seem appropriate. You have had, or will have, other opportunities to speak so sit back, relax, and allow the "Senior Person" to go ahead and sell the company. Many will ask you very few questions other than probably the easiest to ask and the most difficult one to answer: "Tell me about yourself".

Answering the "Tell me about yourself" question

Almost all the recent graduates surveyed said this was the most difficult question they encountered in their recruiting process. Experienced people have no less trouble with this seemingly innocuous question. Take a recent interviewee, for example. The gentleman in question had been with the same company for twenty years and had worked his way steadily up the ladder. At the beginning of the interview, I asked the infamous question: "Tell me about yourself". Forty-five seconds later, he was finished. It was sad to think that anyone could summarize twenty years of his life in forty five seconds. I asked him the question again, suggesting he expand on what he said and take as much time as he needed. This time, it took him three minutes.

In another example, a student recently seem stunned by the question, but she gathered herself together and responded: "I am dynamic and vivacious. I have excellent people skills and I am very intelligent I think sometimes I am… I suppose". Remember what I said about qualifiers in the chapter on interviewing. Was she intelligent or not? She said she was, but then went on to say she was only intelligent sometimes.

There are significant lessons to be learned from these two stories. Practice answering this question and make sure you have versions that will last anywhere from three to fifteen minutes. Immediately upon being asked the question, ask the interviewer how long you should take in answering, make the necessary adjustments in your mind and go for it. Nothing will impress an interviewer more than a well organized, interesting "autobiography" where your skills and experience are geared towards the position for which you are interviewing.

This is the one question that you can answer and ensure you have covered everything on your "Best Qualities Card".

Group Interviews

While these are not common, one of the recent graduates surveyed shared the following experience with us:

> "When I went into my second interview, 6 interviewers and two other interviewees were in the room. They first gave us background information and showed us a film on the company. Then the interviewers put all the interviewees at one end of the conference table while they moved to the other end. One of the interviewers explained that we were going to get a list: 5 names, 5 occupations, 5 bank names, 5 bank account numbers and 5 bank balances. We also got 12 slips of paper that had clues written on them. With this information we were, as a group, to determine which name went with which occupation, bank balance, etc. We were given an easel, chart paper, and a marker and we were told to solve the problem, while we were being watched from the other end of the table."

> Lorie Gibson, Accountant/Analyst, DuPont Canada Inc.,
> Wilfrid Laurier University Grad '94

*There are
so many things
you can learn about.
BUT... you'll miss
the best things
if you keep
your eyes shut.*

Dr Seuss

If you find yourself in this or a similar scenario, immediately assume that you and all the other interviewees will be hired and treat them as if they are your future colleagues. Don't hesitate to give your opinion, but make sure you listen to and respect the views of other interviewees. Keep in mind throughout the exercise that the interviewers will be assessing your interpersonal skills, your leadership potential and your ability to be a productive member of a team. Make sure you don't shine in one of these assessment areas and fail in others because you tried too hard to impress.

Tour of premises or facilities

These are usually conducted by either technical people, if it is a technical facility or a young recent graduate, if it is not. Stay alert and ask questions. The impression that you want to leave is that you were interested and enthusiastic. Granted, it is far easier to be interested and ask questions when touring a manufacturing facility than a series of offices but appear interested nonetheless. You will probably be introduced to people along the way. The usual rules apply. Shake their hand firmly, look them in the eye and if appropriate, ask them a question about their particular area of involvement. You'll be amazed how often those brief comments that line managers make like "he seems like a bright guy" or "she appears to very sharp", following a very brief meeting on a tour, will have a positive effect on the final decision makers. If it is a production facility you are visiting, your research into the company should give you enough information about the technical processes to ask appropriate questions.

Getting a feel for the corporate culture

Your visit to the organization provides you with the perfect opportunity to get a feel for the corporate culture, as well as an affinity for the people and the atmosphere. Keep your eyes and ears open. Try to get a feel for the interaction between people in the organization. Take note of these factors:

Is the atmosphere warm, cold or somewhere in between?

Observe the interaction between staff and management. Is it warm and friendly, cold and forced, or somewhere in between?

Where do entry level people sit? Does it look comfortable? Have they given it a personal touch?

How up-to-date is the technology?

What impression did you get from the washrooms?

Is the workplace clean? Orderly? Are most people's desks disorganized or neatly arranged?

What are the arrangements for parking?

Come prepared to 'blow your own horn'. Tell employers about past success – it will be your only chance.

Kelly Smith
Regional Manager,
London Life Insurance Co.

Does it look like a safe place to work weekends and nights?

What do people do at lunch time? Where?

What impression did you get from the in-house newspapers and corporate literature?

Remember, you need to answer a lot of questions about the aforementioned facts in order to do a meaningful comparison of your offers.

Cocktail receptions

In an earlier chapter, I discussed cocktail parties. Most of my previous comments apply to in-house receptions as well. The primary difference is obviously that all the hosts at an in-house cocktail party are from the organization you are visiting.

Make sure you circulate and talk to as many people as possible. It's another excellent opportunity to ask questions and get a feel for the company's atmosphere. Try not to spend too long with any one group of people. After all, you want to meet as many people as possible. If you find yourself in a group that includes very senior people as well as recent graduate employees, make sure you don't ignore anyone. Too many people fix their attention on the senior people and snub the recent hires. Don't. Observe the interaction between the recent graduates and their superiors. While some of their behaviour may be staged for the event, chances are the interplay will be real.

I am asked regularly by students if it is alright to drink alcohol during recruiting functions. Let me begin by saying that it is perfectly acceptable not to drink alcohol. For those of you who don't drink, or for those of you who choose not to at business events, have a soft drink or water.

I do suggest you have a glass in your hand. You'll probably get very thirsty and an empty glass that needs refilling is a great way to get away from someone with whom you've finished talking. If you want to drink alcohol, go ahead and have one drink. But limit it to one. You want to stay at the top of your game every step of the way. Even if your hosts try to persuade you to have another, decline politely.

Meals

If you are fortunate enough to be taken out for lunch or dinner as part of the process, you'll have an excellent meal at a fine restaurant, but there is a price to pay. Not your share of the bill – your host will take care of that – but the potential employer has yet another opportunity to observe and assess you in what might be unfamiliar territory for you.

Some general guidelines to follow with respect to dining out:

1. Wait to be told where to sit. Your host will probably have a seating plan in mind and will place you.

2. Remove your napkin immediately. It's either in front of you or on your left, open it and place it on your lap.

3. The next thing that is likely to happen is that the waiter will bring you a menu or one may have been left on the table in front of you. Don't open it until your host has.

4. Next, the waiter arrives to take your drink orders. In most cases, the polite host will ask you what you are going to have. Don't be the first to order alcohol. If everyone else does, you certainly may have one drink. If not, play it safe and order a soft drink or water. No one will think it strange.

5. Ordering food comes next. Once again, it may be up to you to order first so be prepared. Make a decision. Even at this stage, and with something seemingly unrelated to work, you don't want to be seen as indecisive. I suggest you choose something that is neither the cheapest nor the most expensive item on the menu. Make it something you are going to eat and enjoy and not something that you order just because everyone else does. If you don't enjoy your food and leave half of it, your host will feel uncomfortable. Order something you will eat enthusiastically and you will finish. Don't criticize the food, the service or the restaurant even if your hosts do. You don't want to be seen as a griper. After all, you're not paying and you did not choose the restaurant. Avoid food like spaghetti that may end up splattering your clothes. Food that is traditionally eaten with your hands, like lobster, ribs, and crab legs should also be avoided.

At the end of each course, indicate that you have finished eating by placing your utensils parallel to each other on your plate.

It is not necessary to offer to pay for the meal or leave the tip. At the end of your meal simply thank the organization representatives for their hospitality and let them know you appreciated the opportunity to spend more time with them.

Enjoy them!!! Remember them!!

Scott Gregory
Manager of Career Services,
Faculty of Administration,
University of Ottawa

Other do's and don'ts of business meals

DO read this list before venturing out to your first recruiting meal.

DO wait until your host tells you where to sit.

DO learn which utensils to use during which course. Traditionally, you begin with the utensils on the outside and work your way in. For example, the smaller, outside fork (on the left) is used first for the salad. Likewise, the large, outer spoon (on the right) is used for the soup. Finally, the large fork (on the left) and the large knife (on the right) are used for the main meal. The small spoon, often at the top of your plate, is used for dessert. Remember that your bread plate is to your left. Your napkin is the one immediately in front of you or just to your left. Your wine and water glasses will also be either immediately in front of you or just to your right.

DO indicate that you are finished eating by placing your utensils parallel to each other on your plate.

DO offer your napkin with your apologies if you happen to spill something on someone.

DO keep your free hand on your lap or your wrist on the edge of the table.

DO mention that you found the food and/or service particularly good once the meal has ended.

DON'T arrive at the restaurant with gum in your mouth. If you have a cloth napkin, you may have no discrete place to put it.

DON'T place your purse or agenda book on the table. You should put it in your lap or on the floor between your feet.

DON'T smoke. If your host has already lit a cigarette, go ahead, but remember it will turn some people off. Don't ever ask for permission to smoke.

DON'T begin eating until everyone has been served. If it takes much longer for some people to get their meals, the polite host may tell you that you should not wait for fear your meal will get cold.

DON'T chew with your mouth open or speak while your mouth is full.

DON'T announce how "stuffed" you are at the end of the meal.

DON'T reapply your lipstick, comb your hair or pick food from your teeth at the table. Always excuse yourself and go to the washroom.

DON'T relax too much. Remember that you are still being interviewed.

Relax – don't be nervous, be prepared to answer questions about 'why we should hire you'. Close the sale – make us love you!

Mike Tuff
Coordinator,
Education & Training,
The Toronto-Dominion Bank

Reimburseable expenses

If you are travelling out of town for an interview and the visit involves an overnight stay, do not abuse your host's hospitality. Do not use the mini-bar in the hotel room, watch a movie or invite a friend over to have a meal with you. A few years ago, a student we were seriously considering hiring spent $200 in the mini-bar and on breakfast for four people. When we received the bill from the hotel the next day, we immediately sent him a rejection letter.

Interviews... What Not to Discuss or Ask

Salary

Do not ask about the salary during the first interview unless the interviewer brings it up. This applies even if you know for certain that there will not be another round of interviews. You do not want the interviewer to think that the dollar sign is more important to you than the job itself. Wait until the organization makes you an offer. Then you'll be in a far better position to negotiate, knowing that they really want you. Your research will probably have provided you with all the information you need about what you're expected to earn. If you're asked, always give a range rather than an exact number. If you are an engineer or accountant, for example, make sure you have researched the industry standards and mention these if you are asked what you are expecting to earn.

Know what you need to know

Do not ask questions that will demonstrate your lack of research about the firm. Frequent examples such as "in what cities do you have offices?" or "how many people do you employ?" should be avoided. You should know this without having to ask it in an interview! As a guideline, before you ask the question, decide whether you could have found the information by doing research. Many companies will, in fact, ask you if you have any questions about the organization just to test the quality of the research you have done. Use the research you've done to prepare a series of questions based on your assessment of the research. They will be far more impressed if you ask about their philosophies and mission statement or if you make comments about their plans for future expansion, planned new markets or products. Not only will this indicate your research ability, but that you are genuinely interested in their organization.

Turning the tables on the interviewers

Don't turn the tables on an interviewer by saying "Tell me a little bit about your background". You don't want them to be put on the spot.

Generic questions

Many students are intent on finding a generic question and asking it to each and every interviewer. Those questions often sound fake and are far too often asked out of context. Questions, like resumes and cover letters, should be tailored to each interview and should only be asked if you genuinely want to know something.

Criticizing the organization or interviewer

Never criticise the company. For example: "Why would your organization only arbitrarily give bonuses to some employees? That doesn't seem fair to the others".

Never compare it with another company. For example, avoid saying "Well, when I worked at company X, they certainly didn't do things that way".

Likelihood of success

Do not ask anyone you meet during the process, what your chances are of getting the job. Even in the most seemingly informal settings, like cocktail parties or lunches, don't sound desperate. You don't want to ever put the interviewer or anyone else in the organization on the spot.

Negative qualities

Far too many students portray a negative image, as much by the way they answer questions, as by the actual questions they ask:

"Are there many late nights in the office?
"Will I have to work on weekends?"
"Will there be many menial tasks?"
"Will I be out of town a lot?"

142

There should be no need to ask questions like these because this information should be forthcoming in the research you've done. If not, and you haven't been told specifically about these expectations, ask the questions but do so in a positive way. For example, "Can you tell me how much travelling a typical new graduate will do in a year?"

Further studies

If you've done your research correctly, you know what the organization's attitude is towards further education and more specifically, how they may feel about your leaving them in a few years to pursue further studies. Unless they are one of the few who will encourage or even sponsor this, never discuss future school plans with a potential employer. Just remember how much time and money they are investing in your orientation, adaptation and training.

Don't mention your faults

A frequently asked question in an interview is "what are your weaknesses?" This is a tough question because the last thing you want the company to find out about is your biggest fault, when you've spent the entire interview trying to sell them on your strengths and why they should hire you.

A recent interviewee applying for an entry level position in Human Resources told me that one of her weaknesses was that she didn't have any close friends because she didn't get along well with people.

Another person, interviewing for an entry level administrative position, revealed to me that his biggest weakness was that he was not very organized. In both cases, the interviewees were being honest. Unfortunately, all it got them was a rejection letter. I am not suggesting that you lie. What I am suggesting is that there is no way to answer this type of question well. No one will ever be able to say you didn't give the "right" answer. Make sure that the weakness, or fault, that you reveal is not work-related. I asked the graduate who told me she didn't get along well with people whether or not, in my position, she would hire someone with that weakness for a Human Resources position that required constant people contact. She saw my point.

Revealing the fact that you have poor interpersonal skills

Whenever you are dealing with reasons for leaving a previous job, organization, club or committee, try to come up with positive reasons for why you left. The fact that you did not get along with co-workers or superiors will make interviewers extremely nervous. Avoid any reference to the fact that you may be difficult to get along with.

Making conversation

Don't ask too many questions just for the sake of asking them or to keep the conversation going. My advice is that you ask as many as you feel you need to, in order to have what you need to know answered. If the interviewer is getting bored or is rushed for time you will know from reading their body language. Remember, in the first interview of a series of interviews, there will be further opportunities, so you don't need to find out everything at once.

Follow up

It is crucial for you to develop a routine to follow at the end of each of your interviews. Whether you are one of the fortunate people who is being selected by everyone to whom you apply or you only have a couple of interviews, the advice that follows is equally important.

Just before the end

It will be the responsibility of the interviewer to conclude the interview. Do not look at your watch under any circumstances; it will send a message to the interviewer that you would like the interview to end. If you are in the habit of constantly looking at you watch, take it off before you go into the interview. To conclude the interview, most interviewers will explain the next step in the process. If you are genuinely interested in the organization, now is the time to let the interviewers know. Shake the recruiters hand and while doing so, state the fact that you are interested and say why. Think of this the same way as a lawyer would think of his or her closing argument in court. Make it short, with impact and sincerity. It will leave the interviewer with a good impression. That's what it is all about.

Taking notes

Most people I know are uncomfortable taking notes in an interview. If you fall into this category it is essential that you follow this post interview routine.

Prior to the interview, prepare a list of questions you have about the organization. Ensure that each of these is answered in the interview. The interviewers will provide you with vital information about the organization that is not in any literature or research you've uncovered. All this information must be added to your fact sheet on the organization. If you took notes in the interview, they should be transcribed into the databank you have developed on the organization. If you're like most people and you rely on your memory, it is essential that you try to remember everything the interviewer told you and make notes immediately following the interview.

Post-interview letters

It is important that you write and thank the interviewers for the interview. It provides you with the perfect opportunity to reaffirm your interest and to re-establish your candidacy. They may have seen twenty or thirty candidates since your interview; it's a good way to remind them about you.

On the following page is an example of an interview follow up letter:

Mr. Peter Tunsay
Director, Human Resources
Saskatchewan Technology Inc.
376 Harrod Road
Saskatoon, Saskatchewan
S7Y 8J9

February 26, 1996

Dear Mr. Tunsay,

Thank you for giving me the opportunity to discuss your opening for a Computer Consultant. I truly enjoyed meeting with you and Ms. Reid and learning more about Saskatchewan Technology Inc.

I was particularly impressed with the atmosphere at your organization. During the company tour, everyone seemed warm and I enjoyed having the chance to interact with them. I feel that this is the type of environment in which I would perform extremely well.

I look forward to hearing from you. Please call me if I can provide more information or answer any questions to assist you with your decision.

Sincerely,

Heidi Adams

Heidi Adams

When to follow up

If the organization has told you when you can expect to hear from them, you are going to have to be patient and wait until that time. It can be nerve-racking but hang in there. If they said they were not sure when they would get back to you, the wait may be even longer. If you have another offer deadline approaching, call the organization and follow the steps discussed in the chapter on job offers. If you do not have a deadline, wait at least two weeks, then call. Once again, express your interest and ask if a decision has been made or when you might expect to hear from them. Make sure you are professional and self confident, they are probably in the process of making their final decision.

Write letters to interviewers expressing your interest.

Linda Ficko
Marketing Analyst / Product Development, TransAlta Utilities Corporation, University of Saskatchewan Grad '94

Assessing Offers

8

Making That Crucial Decision

Congratulations are pouring in. You have just received your first job offer and all those you know are thrilled for you. Those friends who are also in the job market, who didn't buy this book and are still looking for a job, are perhaps a little jealous. Rather than being the end of the process however, the receipt of that first offer is just the beginning of your journey into the working world.

While it will be a decision that you ultimately will have to make yourself, this chapter will assist you in the difficult process of making that decision.

Should you immediately accept the first offer?

Definitely not. Even if it is going to be your only offer, you need to give it careful consideration before accepting. The advice that follows, with respect to comparing offers, applies equally whether you accept a position or not.

CACEE standards of practice require that students who go through fall on-campus recruiting be given until January 15 to respond to job offers. The deadline for students being recruited at other times of the year is four weeks after job offers have been made. The reality of the situation is that not all employers are members of CACEE and therefore will not necessarily abide by these practices.

Some will pressure you into giving them an answer immediately or at best, within a very short period.

What if you are still waiting to hear from other employers? What if you just want to take some time to think about the decision? It is perfectly acceptable to explain your position to an employer. If you have a problem, elaborate on its exact nature. If you still find yourself in a bind, ask the career centre at your institution to assist you in dealing with the employer. Undoubtedly, with their assistance, you will be given the appropriate amount of time to make the right decision. If you haven't heard from an employer in

Like marriage, partnership with the right company will result in a long, successful and satisfying relationship.

Sue Riddell
Manager, Employment & Staffing,
DuPont Canada Inc.

149

Ask questions if you're not sure what something really means.

Doreen Knol
Manager, Engineering Career
Services, McMaster University

Read offers very carefully as they contain very important information about your future. Don't be afraid to contact the company if you feel it's necessary as they may just send out standard offers.

Shelly Broad
Financial Forecast Analyst,
Union Gas Ltd., Wilfrid Laurier
University Grad '94

whom you are still interested, don't hesitate to call them to ask if you are still in the running and when you can expect to hear from them. It certainly won't hurt your chances. In fact, it will let the employer know you are interested in the company and that you have the self confidence to pursue your ambitions.

Go with your gut

As you will have seen from the quotes from recent graduates, many recommend that you "go with your gut". While I agree with this advice in principal, I believe it only applies once you have established which offers meet your expectations and you have eliminated those that do not. Your gut feeling is a great decision advisor if you are finally left with two equal offers.

Assessing and comparing offers

The table at the end of this section is extremely useful for assessing and comparing offers and assisting you in choosing the right one. The criteria listed down the left side column are given only as guidelines. You should eliminate those that don't apply to you and add those that do. Most of the students who've used this chart have found it really useful.

How to use the assessment chart

Think carefully about each of the criteria listed in the first column (after adding your own and deleting those that aren't applicable). Give each one a score on a scale of one to ten, ten being the most important factor for you. Do it in one sitting, then put the chart away.

Some time later, without looking at your first set of results, redo the exercise, then take the average of the two sets of weighting factors. Put this score in the "Rating Column".

Then, think carefully about each of the offers you have received and score each of the criteria on a scale of one to ten, ten being the highest rating again.

If you feel you don't have enough information to assess one of the factors, do everything you can to get the answers. If it is factual information you need, go out and get the facts. If it is a qualitative factor or a personal preference or a lifestyle decision, take your time and do the necessary research. Brainstorm with your family and friends until you feel comfortable

150

with the score you are assigning to the criteria. Do the exercise twice. Reevaluate each factor, without looking at the previous scoring and again, use the average of the two scores to apply to your final assessment. Put these scores under "Org A", "Org B" and so on. The total score for an organization is calculated by multiplying the "Rating" factor by the "Org A" score and putting this number in the "Org A Total" column and by adding up the "Org A Total" column.

Does the organization with the highest score win? The easy answer would be yes. But try this. Eliminate those offers that score well below the top two. If the top scoring organizations are very close I have one suggestion before you let your "gut feeling" make the decision. Contact each of the organizations once more. If it is geographically practical, try to visit them. Remember you have the offer in hand, so be open and honest with them. You have nothing to lose at this stage and everything to gain. Meet with your best contact at the organization and try your best to resolve everything that is still of concern to you. Ask all the tough questions and if the decision comes down to a couple of issues, make sure you have as much information as possible.

Just remember – don't expect anyone to make this decision for you. You are the one who is going to have to work for the organization. Don't be overly influenced by where your friends are going to work.

Make the decision yourself… for you.

Fully understand compensation, particularly "variable" compensation, which goes beyond base salary.

Vici Cox
Analyst, Campus Recruitment,
PanCanadian Petroleum Limited

Take into account all variables such as continuing education, city, salary, benefits, transportation and working environment. Do a cost/benefits analysis before accepting.

Rachelle Kowal
Business Analyst, TransAlta
Utilities Corporation, University
of Saskatchewan Grad '95

The Assessment Chart

Criteria	Rating Factor	Org A	Org A Total	Org B	Org B Total	Org C	Org C Total
1. Chance for promotion and growth							
2. Work that keeps you stimulated							
3. Opportunity for increasing responsibility							
4. Good working conditions							
5. Feeling a part of a team							
6. Full appreciation for work done							
7. Job security							
8. Training program							
9. Loyalty to employees							
10. Nice people to work with							
11. Access to superiors							
12. Geographical location							
13. Empathetic help with personal problems							
14. Starting salary							
15. Potential for salary increases							
16. Corporate culture							
17. Fringe benefits							
18. Possibility of transfers							
19. Vacations							
20. Long Term value to resume							
21. Evaluation system							
22. Social atmosphere							
23. Potential for learning new skills							
24. Potential to receive bonuses							
TOTAL SCORE							

Negotiating the Deal

It is no secret that during the last few years jobs have become increasingly hard to find. With the supply of students out-weighing the demand for them, many students feel that they are in a "take it or lose it" situation.

But once you've landed the job offer, don't let the ecstasy of employment dull your senses to a crucial aspect of career planning – the art of the deal.

Many people believe that negotiating the terms of an employment contract is only for agents of high draft picks of professional sports teams. Nothing could be further from reality. While the ball seems to be in the court of the employer in terms of making the concrete offer, you do have a role to play in ensuring that you get a fair deal. Every aspect of the job and the expectations of both parties should be understood and clearly laid out. If you are not sure what's expected of you, clarify the situation before starting work. Unfortunately, far too many employers do not end up delivering what they promise and far too many new employees fail to live up to expectations. This can be attributed to a number of factors: unrealistic expectations of employees, misrepresentation by employers or simply employers' inexperience at hiring graduating students as new employees. The bottom line is that both parties need to be perfectly clear on their mutual expectations.

The following issues must be covered in the negotiations leading up to employment:

Training
Will there be formal training programs?
Is there on-the-job training?
How long will it last?
Will there be on-going training at each and every level?
At whose expense?
What is the policy with respect to tuition reimbursements for studying that you do outside the workplace?

Travelling
How much will be involved?
What expenses will be covered?

Be prepared to relocate – take a risk.

Pat Chatelain
Campus Recruitment Coordinator,
Syncrude Canada Ltd.

If you get a bad taste in your gut that you would not want to work with the people who interview you… don't take the job.

Rachelle Kowal
Business Analyst, TransAlta
Utilities Corporation, University
of Saskatchewan Grad '95

Will it be over weekends?

How and when are you reimbursed?

Compensation

How much will you be paid?

When will you be paid?

If commissions or bonuses are involved, how are they calculated and when are they paid?

When are salaries reviewed?

How often?

By whom?

Terms of employment

Is there a probation period ?

Is a start date stipulated ?

Is it flexible ?

Career development

Your expected career path should be discussed. This will seldom be given to you in writing but it should be discussed and the expectations clearly expressed.

Will you receive written evaluations ?

How often will these take place ?

Who will prepare them ?

Benefits, sick leave and vacation allowances

These should be spelled out clearly in the offer letter or in the organization's Human Resources Policy Manual.

A job offer is reason to celebrate, but negotiating the right deal can be a complex process. You should enter these negotiations with confidence remembering that they wouldn't have offered you the job if they didn't want to hire you.

One of the most complex terms of employment to negotiate is salary. Fortunately, many organizations experienced at hiring graduating students make life "easy" by having a set salary for all new hires. This may be either a scale they have set themselves or an industry-wide scale. Does this mean

Over salary, benefits, company location and reputation, a position which will give you the opportunity to attain your goals is the one you should choose.

Patrick Farajian
Network Designer, Bell Northern Research
McGill University Grad '94

Go with your instinct.

Marie-Josée Letendre
Audit Intermediate,
Richter, Usher & Vineberg
University of Montreal Grad '93

154

that there is no room to negotiate with these employers? Not at all. What it does mean is that there is less room to negotiate and it will take extraordinary circumstances to warrant breaking from the norm. These may be a special skill that you possess or particularly relevant experience. These special qualities apply equally to employers who do not have preset salary scales.

It will be up to your powers of persuasion to convince the employer that you warrant additional compensation. Is this a dangerous tactic? This will depend on two factors:

Your research into the industry and position will have given you insight into the salary structure.

You have to decide how much you believe the employer really wants you. This is a judgement call and will be dependant on each circumstance. This will determine how much negotiating leeway you have.

My advice is that you think long term and weigh each offer in terms other than monetary. Of course you need sufficient money on which to live, and there is a certain amount of personal satisfaction that goes along with knowing you are earning a good salary. But remember the importance of building the foundation of your long term career over a small short term financial gain.

Restrictive clauses

In some circumstances, offer letters will contain complex, restrictive clauses. These may include, amongst other things, conditions placed on future employment and proprietary knowledge you may acquire. I strongly suggest that in cases such as these, you consult a labour lawyer prior to signing the offer. Most lawyers will charge students only a nominal fee to review an offer letter and it will be well worth the money. Even if the employer tells you it is their standard employment contract, you should still have it checked out if you are concerned about any of the terms in the offer letter.

In every circumstance, insist that the offer be in writing. It should include all the factors discussed in this chapter. Any issues not covered could potentially cause misunderstandings or conflicts once the job has started.

Neither the employer nor the new employee benefit if there is confusion over conditions of the job offer. A clear understanding of expectations on both sides will go a long way in ensuring that the relationship begins on a

Weigh your options, don't say yes to the first offer, just because it was offered to you.

Katherine Ross
Branch Assistant Manager,
The Toronto-Dominion Bank,
University of Calgary Grad '94

A final decision should always consider your long range goals or plans and not just the short term ones.

Mark Throckmorton
Junior Electrical Engineer,
Syncrude Canada Limited,
University of Alberta Grad '92

solid foundation and if it one day must end, it also does so as pleasantly and with as few complications as possible.

Accepting and Rejecting Offers

Be creative in how you augment the traditional sources of information. Want to work for Honda? Go talk to a few Honda dealers – see what they have to say about both the product and their relationship with the manufacturer.

Jim Kelly
Director, Career Planning & Placement, Queen's University

The acceptance of an offer is the most pleasurable part of the entire process. Enjoy it. My advice is simple and easy. Phone the person who sent you the offer letter to accept. In addition, you should also call any other people in the organization whom you got to know well. Remember, you can never have too many allies in the organization and it's never too soon to start building relationships.

If you are sent a contract or offer letter to be signed, it should be returned promptly. In the absence of a formal contract, confirm your acceptance in writing. If there are any aspects of the terms of employment that you wish to clarify, this is the perfect time to do so. This may include your start date and reporting arrangements.

Rejecting the other offers you have received is the final part of the recruiting process. Too many people do not do this very well and all too often, it comes back to haunt them.

You should let all the employers who have made you offers know as soon as possible after you've accepted an offer. This quick response will help other students who might get an offer sooner because of your decision. Your rejections should be just as professional as your acceptances.

Look to the longer term rather than the first job.

Bruce Walker
Coordinator, Recruitment, Union Gas Ltd.

You can communicate your decision either in a letter or in person. Either way, it is essential that you let the organization know. You have no obligation to tell the organization why you are rejecting the offer. It is up to you how to respond, if you are asked. Just remember throughout the rejection process that one day, you may want to work for the organization you are now rejecting, or for the person or people who were involved in the recruiting process.

About four years ago, I made an offer to a student whom we never heard from again, despite numerous attempts to reach her. Recently, she applied for a senior position in the same organization she had previously chosen to slight. She paid the ultimate price for her earlier transgression and did not receive an interview. By contrast, a year or two earlier, a student who was offered a position decided to reject the offer in person explaining, in detail, why she had accepted another offer. Each year, from that time on, she sent a seasons' greeting card to those who had been involved in the recruiting process. Many years later, when the organization advertised for a management level opening, she felt comfortable enough to call her contacts and apply directly. They remembered her professionalism and made sure she received an interview.

She got the job.

Pick a company you feel you will fit into. Take a job you feel will benefit your future career.

Shelly Broad
Financial Forecast Analyst,
Union Gas Ltd.,
Wilfrid Laurier University Grad '94

What Recruiters Really Want

9

To enable me to provide you with advice that is current and reflects the views of recruiters from a broad array of organizations, I surveyed employers from across Canada. The following is a summary of their responses.

In general terms, what are you looking for in a student?

Enthusiasm	Technical proficiency
Ambition	High energy level
Curiosity	Honesty
Excellent communication skills	History of success
Relevant work experience	Independence
Experience with teams	Judgement
Good GPA	Adaptability
Motivation	Professionalism
Initiative	Attention to detail
Willingness to accept change	Leadership
Creativity	

What advice can you give to graduating students with respect to:

a) Career fairs?

Speak to as many recruiters as possible.

Attend them, they are an excellent opportunity to find out more about the companies.

Look presentable.

Talk to people, try to make them remember you.

Be prepared to look at each and every company as a potential opportunity.

Ask recruiters as many questions as possible regarding all aspects of their organization and what will be done to assist the recent graduate.

Plan ahead and prepare your questions and think about what you want to achieve from visiting with companies.

b) Resumes/CACEE (ACCIS) forms?

Must be typed.

No spelling mistakes.

Brief but explicit enough.

Remember this is the first opportunity that an employer gets to "see" you, therefore pay particular attention to spelling, grammar ensureing the information is accurate i.e. Company name, etc.

Be clear and concise.

Relate your qualifications and experience as much as possible to the job requirements.

Be specific with respect to career objective – state your real interests – not "a job where I can apply my skills".

c) Networking?

Be aware of current affairs… i.e. economic trends and current issues affecting the company.

Extremely important, but don't be too pushy about it.

Get to know people and call regularly.

Always be positive and friendly.

Start early, keep contact.

Remain in contact with college and university professors and friends.

Make it an objective at each event you attend that you add at least one person to your contact list.

Record on their business card where you met the person and how you could help them and they could help you.

d) First interviews?

Research the company.

Appear confident.

Prepare, prepare, prepare.

Come prepared to "Blow your own horn". Tell employers about past success – it may be your only chance.

Be on time.

Be prepared with questions.

Be yourself – the rest will come naturally.

Don't try too hard, try to relax and provide the best answer you can think of.

Anticipate questions related to the job and based on experience as it applies to the job (structural, behavioural-based interviews).

Be prepared to answer questions about "why we should hire you".

e) Second interviews?

Research the position.

This is where you are interviewed by the hiring manager.

More "technically" oriented interview – main focus on what you know and what you can contribute.

Know who you are interviewing with and where they fit in.

Be prepared to distinguish yourself from others, particularly with your "soft" skills.

Close the sale – make us love you!

f) Making final decisions?

Make sure the job is what you are looking for.

Look at all your options carefully, think of your career goals – where you'd like to be in 3 to 5 years.

Don't just focus on "how much money I can make".

Be prepared to relocate – take a risk.

Look to the longer term.

Have lots of choices. Don't restrict yourself.

Fully understand compensation, particularly "variable" compensation.

Make sure you are comfortable with the company, its values and philosophy.

Do your homework so that if an offer comes your way you will be prepared to accept/reject it in the period of time provided to you by the employer.

g) Job offers?

Money should not be the main deciding factor. Look for growth.

Review your job offer carefully.

Get back to the company by the deadline.

Don't burn any bridges.

Be absolutely certain to take everything into account.

Respond as quickly as possible to job offers – this allows other offers to be made to your classmates!

This is the best time to negotiate.

What really turns you off a student?

Lack of professionalism.

If they don't know anything at all about our company – are they really interested in us?

Being late.

Lack of interest.

Lack of preparation.

Taking company for granted.

Self confidence is good – but don't go over the line.

Someone who constantly interrupts an interviewer.

Someone who defensively asks why a question was asked when it is clearly based on a bona fide job related criteria.

Lack of focus regarding career.

The Job Search Experience
of Recent Graduates

10

We surveyed recent graduates from a wide variety of disciplines about their job search experiences. They are currently working for organizations across the country. The following is a summary of their responses.

What was the toughest part of getting a job?

Waiting for a response from an employer after an interview.
Trying to decide between two job offers.
All the rejection letters.
The amount of time and effort required to prepare resumes/ACCIS forms, research jobs, check job board, prepare for interviews.
Finding a job that is a "good fit" for you.
Distinguishing yourself from the other candidates.
Finding companies that were hiring in your field.
Balancing school, extracurricular activities, working and concentrating on doing well with interviews during the recruitment process, was very difficult during the fall semester.
Getting information on companies.
The time and energy involved in the recruiting process.
Conversing with the various representatives.
Knowing what I wanted to do without having experienced it.
Being older than the typical graduate and getting an entry level job.
Development of an "attention-grabbing" resume and cover letter.
The waiting and the wondering.

What advice can you give to graduating students with respect to:

a) **Career fairs?**
Attend career fairs because they are the perfect opportunity to meet recruiters and learn first hand exactly what the company is about.

You learn exactly what kind of skills and employee profiles companies are after. Attend as many as you can.

Get their (the recruiters) names and/or business card and mention that you spoke to them at the fair when you write your cover letter.

Be confident.

Do homework on the companies in which you are interested.

Know which companies will be there, before you go.

Attend career fairs because you are often asked during an interview if you attended.

b) Resumes/CACEE (ACCIS) forms?

Target each cover letter and resume… to do so, research as much as possible and demonstrate your knowledge in your application.

Emphasize leadership and communication skills, since these are more important than simply a high GPA.

Emphasize technical skills acquired outside of courses. If you don't have much, emphasize skills you obtained in the courses rather than just naming them.

Start early! Spend a lot of time on it.

You can never proof read it too many times.

Show the employer how you can benefit them.

Make valuable use of the last page on the ACCIS form where you can add any relevant information

Be truthful because every detail will be brought out in the interview process.

Keep in mind that you somehow have to make yourself stand out from the rest of the crowd.

Highlight skills rather than tasks for past work experience.

Write from your heart, not from "what they want you to say" point of view.

Don't include irrelevant information.

c) Networking?

It always helps to get your foot in the door through an established contact.

If you are reluctant to do so, keep in mind that others are not.

Give your resume to people that you know in companies that are of interest to you.

Keep in touch with friends. They might be able to alert you to job openings in their companies.

Don't look desperate to those with whom you are networking.

The best place to start is at the career fair. The recruiters will remember strong candidates and will look for your resume later!

This is in my opinion, the most important tool in obtaining any job and is certainly the reason I have mine.

Keep in contact with your graduating classmates... you never know when they'll be in a position to assist you.

d) First interviews?

Prepare answers to commonly asked questions in order to boost your confidence at the interview.

Try as much as possible not to show how nervous you really are.

Be confident.

Maintain eye contact.

Think before you speak.

If there is more than one person interviewing you, make sure you respond to both, no matter which person asked you the question.

Show a keen interest in wanting to learn more about the company.

Know your resume backwards and forwards.

Don't be afraid to bring out a point you feel is important if they don't.

Be yourself. If they don't like you for who you are, then the employer is probably not a good fit for you.

Practice with someone before you go into an interview.

If the interviewer is someone from the Human Resources Department do not use technical mumbo-jumbo; explain your work in terms that your parents could understand.

Take a few seconds to think about your response before you give it.

In a behavioural-interviewing setting, if you have never experienced what they are asking, answer by saying "what you would have done being in that situation".

While skill is very important don't neglect charm and personality.

e)   Second interviews?

Be friendly to everyone you meet.

Ask questions about the operations of the company.

Find out all about the company culture.

Don't sound like you have a script.

This interview is often more technical.

Express your interest in the position.

Ensure that when you leave, you have no unanswered questions about the position.

Try to keep the conversation smooth and continuous.

Know the interviewing company inside and out.

Be able to explain and show what you can do for the company and why they should hire you and why you want to work for them.

Know the future direction of the company and what value you can bring to it.

Research what "attitudes" the company is looking for as opposed to "skills". Obviously the company realizes you can be taught any skill... it is the attitude/character that can not be taught or changed very easily.

f)   Making final decisions?

Have a priority list of values and goals and your final decisions should follow from those priorities.

Always look at the big picture.

Don't be afraid to try something new.

Make sure you like the atmosphere.

Talk to as many people as you can because it helps to get different points of view.

If the job involves relocation, visit the area to get a feel for whether you would enjoy life there.

A final decision should always consider your long range goals or plans and not just the short term ones.

Consider the work environment and your co-workers carefully. You are going to be spending most of your time with these people.

Don't say yes to the first offer.

Don't allow "offerors" to pressure you.

Trust your judgement.

What was the most unusual thing that happened to you during the recruiting process?

I had an interview in which the interviewer did all the talking.

The firm I was most interested in never received my ACCIS form. Luckily I had attended so many recruiting events that the HR people were expecting my form; when they didn't receive it, they called me.

The first question I was asked in an interview was can I play goalie for their hockey team!

Being hired by the company with whom "I felt" I had the worst interview. The difference was a business card given to me at a job fair. Had I not taken the time to meet the person from the company, I may still be job hunting today.

The Vast Experience
of Career Educators

11

By the time you read this chapter I know you will be well known to everyone at your Career Centre. As part of the research for this book, I surveyed Career Educators from across Canada so that you could benefit from the collective wisdom of their vast experience. The following is a summary of their responses.

What advice can you give to graduating students with respect to:

a) **Career Fairs?**

Research the organization in which you have an interest, prior to attending a career fair.

Go to the fair prepared to ask questions and make a positive impression.

Go to every career fair you can possibly attend.

View career fairs as an opportunity to pursue your own career investigation.

Find out which companies will be attending and prepare questions.

Career fairs are an excellent networking experience.

Talk to people who might be in the fields that interest you. Ask for their cards and follow up with a letter and resume if there is a "glimmer of hope".

Develop some type of introduction for yourself before going so that you feel comfortable meeting the employers.

Make that first impression count: from the handshake to the polished shoes.

You cannot find another venue that offers such a great opportunity to interact with employers with such limit on the down side risk.

b) **Resumes/CACEE (ACCIS) forms?**

Clearly identify your skills and where you have used them prior to starting to write a resume or CACEE form.

Make your resume come alive with examples of accomplishments and differences your work made.

Write and rewrite and rewrite.

When completing a CACEE form which is being used in conjunction with a resume, make certain the form is complete – do not leave sections incomplete with the notation "see attached resume". This will convey a message of laziness.

Attend a workshop on how to complete one. If you learn even one thing, it may just be what makes the difference.

Spend a lot of time on the last page and sell, sell, sell.

Don't leave completing the ACCIS form to the last minute! It takes a long time to fill out the form correctly.

Give both the resume and cover letter a focus or don't bother sending them. Don't make any errors.

Have at least five people proofread it for you.

Highlight your accomplishments.

c) Doing research on employers?

Read everything available and talk to as many people as you are able.

Never say you couldn't find information.

Be creative in how you augment the traditional sources of information. Want to work for Honda? Go talk to a few Honda dealers – see what they have to say about the product and their relationships with the manufacturer.

Employers know you want a job but they want to know why you want to work for them in particular.

Research provides a base to ask and answer questions in your interview.

Remember research is for your benefit. The time taken to find out about a company indicates enthusiasm and initiative.

Research allows you to compare your interests and goals to that of the company.

d) Networking?

Networking is the foundation for everyone looking for work.

The more people you meet and who are aware of what you have to offer, the more chance you have of finding the type of work you want.

Networking creates opportunity!

Networking means building and maintaining a pool of contacts.

Student clubs are the best way to practice meeting with strangers.

Networking is a necessity in order to tap the "hidden job market".

The labour market lends itself to the networking process since the supply of labour far exceeds the demand and employers are reluctant to publicize their vacancies knowing that the response will be overwhelming.

Develop networking skills so they become part of who you are.

Always be professional and courteous.

Never burn any bridges.

Important and must be on-going with list of contacts expanding regularly.

Networking doesn't have to be a scary thing – develop your own style of networking that you are comfortable with.

e) First interviews?

Research the organization and the position as well as preparing to be able to clearly articulate how your skills and experiences match the requirements.

Prepare knowing that the emphasis will be on interpersonal and communications skills and on the "fit" with the company culture and values.

Confirm interview time and name(s) of interviewer(s).

You may be the most qualified person for the job but if you don't market yourself effectively in the first interview, you won't be the successful candidate.

Rehearse the "top 100 questions".

Know why you applied to the job.

First and often the only impression you get a chance to make.

It is not a rehashing of your resume but an opportunity to sell yourself.

Smile!

Be yourself.

f) Making final decisions?

Consider the long term but remember that nothing is forever.

If you start your job search "knowing what you are looking for" – making the final decision is easy.

Make a list of all the things that are relevant to you in terms of the "ideal" job. (i.e. salary, location, responsibilities, promotion, etc.) Always use this checklist to measure how attractive an offer is to you.

When you have accepted the offer, respond both verbally and in writing.

If unsure, "buy" yourself some time.

Speak to as many people employed in the company as possible.

Remember it's you who will have to live with the decision so don't make it without a great deal of thought.

g) Job offers?

Make sure that you have all the necessary details to make your decision.

Based on these facts (decide) whether the position meets your realistic expectations.

Accepting and declining, both require acknowledgement of receipt and expression of appreciation.

Don't accept until you are sure.

Negotiate fairly and reasonably.

Deal openly and ethically with the potential employers.

Offers must be in writing.

Job offers should comply with CACEE Standards of Practice.

Leave nothing to chance, do not assume - ask.

Don't jump at the first offer – take time to make sure it's the right job for you.

Look at the total package.

Are there any other "Pearls of wisdom" you wish to share with graduating students?

Never, never, never give up looking for a job.

Learning how to look for and secure a job is the most critical higher skill we can acquire.

Target your job search - don't do mass mailings.

Always try to stay positive especially when things look "bleak".

Commit the same amount of energy to yourself and your career pursuits as you would to your academic courses. Don't make yourself second priority.

Receptionists and secretaries are your best friends. They can get you in a locked door, get you the job or block your every move.

There are jobs out there and people get hired every day. There is just much more competition.

Do the homework because job search takes time, patience and hard work but pays off.

Determine as early as possible the career direction that you would like to embark on and focus your energies toward that goal.

Remember in the next century most employment opportunities will be in small companies.

The Canadian Association of
Career Educators and Employers

12

The Canadian Association of Career Educators and Employers (CACEE) is a national, bilingual, non-profit association dedicated to facilitating the process of matching graduates with employment. As a partnership of employer recruiters and career educators, its mission is to provide authoritative information, advice and services to students, employers and career centre personnel in the areas of career planning and student recruitment.

The association was founded in 1946 and has been known in the past as the University and College Placement Association (UCPA) and then ACCIS – The graduate workforce professionals. CACEE is a partnership of business and education working towards a common goal.

This chapter sets out the CACEE standards of practice for recruitment/placement at post-secondary educational institutions. These practices are intended to provide a framework for the professional relationships between employers, students and career counsellors/placement professionals.

Student Responsibilities

It is the student's responsibility to comply with all relevant Federal and Provincial legislation.

With respect to interviews
Prepare for the interview

Provide accurate and appropriate information on your qualifications and interests in the form requested by the employer

Notify the Career Centre well in advance if you must reschedule or cancel interviews

Acknowledge invitations for site visits or second interviews promptly whether you accept or reject them

Notify employers well in advance if you must postpone or cancel site visits or second interviews

Accept interview invitations (second and subsequent) only when seriously considering a position with the employer

With respect to job offers

Discuss offers with employers to verify terms and reach mutually acceptable responses

Notify employers that you are accepting or rejecting an offer as soon as you make your decision

Respond to every offer whether you accept or reject it

Notify the Career Centre immediately upon confirmation of a job acceptance to withdraw from the placement process

Honour your acceptance of the offer as it is a contractual agreement with the employer

Employer Responsibilities

It is the employer's responsibility to comply with all relevant Federal and Provincial legislation.

With respect to interviews

Contact the Career Centre well in advance to reserve interview space

Provide company literature

Notify all applicants individually of their status

Provide accurate information on job responsibilities, compensation and benefits

Interview for positions whose starting dates are within 12 months of the initial interview

Respond to all candidates within agreed upon time frames

Give reasonable notice, at least 3 days, of any interview cancellations

Honour all offers of employment

Advise students what costs will be compensated for site and interview visits

With respect to job offers

Confirm job offers and terms of employment in writing to students

Inform the Career Centre regularly of the status of their campaign

Job offers must be in writing and should comply with the CACEE Standards of Practice for Recruitment/Placement in Canadian Post-Secondary Institutions, with reference to 'recommended job acceptance dates'.

Ernie Hovell
Director, Career Planning &
Employment Centre,
Acadia University

Educational Institutions' Responsibilities

It is the educational institution's responsibility to comply with all relevant Federal and Provincial legislation.

With respect to interviews

Accommodate employers' reasonable requests for job posting and interview space

Ensure that students have reasonable (recommend a minimum of 5 weeks) time from the start of the school year to prepare for the on-campus recruitment process prior to the commencement of interviews

With respect to employment preparation

Provide information, resources and advice to students on career planning and job search

Inform students of acceptable recruitment ethics, procedures and responsibilities

General Issues

Provide equal service to all students and employers

Follow legal and ethical guidelines in providing student information to employers

Bring to the attention of the parties involved any questionable recruitment practices

Job acceptance dates

It is the responsibility of the employer, student and the Career Centre to establish reasonable job acceptance dates. CACEE recommends that job acceptance dates be set with consideration for the type of employment involved and the graduation or availability of the student.

Full time

Graduating students have until January 15th to respond to job offers made in the Fall semester (September to December). A minimum of 4 weeks from the date of the job offer is the recommended amount of time graduating students be given to respond to offers made during the remainder of the year.

Summer

Students have until December 15th to respond to job offers made in the Fall semester (September to December). A minimum of two weeks from the date of the job offer is the recommended amount of time students be given to respond to offers made during the rest of the year.

Exceptions

In certain cases, groups of employers in a particular industry have grouped together to alter the dates and time-frames that are described above. In all such cases your Career Centre will be aware of any such modifications. If you are faced with alternate dates or time-frames, discuss them immediately with your Career Centre.

The Crucial First Year
in the Workplace

13

Congratulations! You have achieved the primary objective of the book and have landed the job you wanted. Before you step into the real world, I'd like to pass along a few of words of advice. Entering the workforce should be a time of excitement, enthusiasm, and exploration for you. School is over. The time has finally come to apply some of the knowledge and insights you've acquired. All kinds of doors are opening to you, presenting a whole new world of opportunities.

The transition from school to career is dramatic. Unfortunately, far too many final year students are not aware of the magnitude of this transition. Adjustments need to be made on virtually all fronts, and many are unaware of the consequences of not making these adjustments. You need to be prepared for this new world and this chapter will be your guide. Its purpose is to present some of the realities and opportunities of a first job. In addition, it should enable you to build a strong foundation for your career and to make the transition successfully and enjoyably.

It is a shock, as a new graduate, to discover you must once again drop to "rookie" status. Just as you had to learn the ropes your first year in kindergarten, high school, college or university, when you start your first career job, you will face a completely new environment. The working world is far less tolerant of mistakes, provides less time and flexibility for adjustment, and demands a consistent, high level of performance and dedication in exchange for the short and long term rewards it offers.

You need to enter this world with your eyes wide open and with enthusiasm, realizing that life will be different from now on.

Oh, the places you'll go!
Congratulations!
Today is your day,
You're off to Great Places!
You're off and away.
You have brains in your head.
You have feet in your shoes.
You can steer yourself in any
direction you choose.
Out here things can happen
and frequently they do
to people as brainy
and footsy as you.

Dr. Seuss

The Transition

The key to your success in the school-to-work transition is the recognition and understanding of the differences between school and work, and your willingness and ability to adjust to them. Wise graduates will recognize the necessary behavioural changes that must be made. Accept them, and thrive on the challenges this new world will present to them.

Dealing with a schedule

University and college life offers you an incredible amount of flexibility in how you spend your time. When you plan your schedule, if you plan your schedule, you have the option of avoiding morning courses, staying up until 3:00 a.m. doing whatever you choose, when you choose. Falling behind in your class work for a week or more then working at a frenzied pace to catch up is not unusual and goes relatively unnoticed. You have had the option of skipping a class or two, then getting notes from a friend. If you did this in college, those days are over.

First of all, you cannot skip work. If your starting time is 8:30, you are advised to arrive early and be ready for action. Excuses for tardiness or absences will not be appreciated and recurring behaviour of this type will result first in a negative image and if chronic, eventually dismissal.

The workplace has little tolerance for the fact that you are "not a morning person". It will not be interested in your late night escapades, or that your car would not start or got stuck in the snow. You are expected to be punctual and ready to perform at your peak from the start of every day. Even if you get more done in six hours than others do in ten, you will be reprimanded for tardiness. Develop a reputation for being early or at least, punctual. One of the easiest ways to make a good impression at your new workplace is to demonstrate consistent punctuality.

Student life allows for mid-day breaks and days off, often at your discretion. You can usually relax and study on your own schedule. Your new job will probably call for you to be working continually through the day. This straight-through schedule can be, for some, a rude awakening. Even if you are working in an environment that is far more relaxed with respect to start times and work schedules, it is recommended that you establish a consistent work pattern. Once you arrive at work you should be prepared to immediately start your day.

Vacation time

It is a good idea to take some time to unwind between graduation and beginning your job. It will probably be your last vacation for a while and certainly your last major (more than two weeks) vacation for a long time. Many jobs will only offer you two weeks vacation per year for the first few years. If you are fortunate enough, you may get three weeks vacation. Either way, you usually cannot take time off until you have worked at least six months.

While you were in school, you became accustomed to long vacations after each semester. Now you find that it's week after week of work with no long breaks, even at the end of a major project. You may be asked to work weekends to meet a tough deadline and again, you probably will not get days off to recuperate.

So, if you are thinking seriously about taking a break, going on that European back-packing vacation or that trip to the far North, go for it. You do not want feelings of regret three months into your first job.

You may well look back enviously on all the free time you had during your school years. Remember it fondly, but do not resent the demands made by your job. You paid for college – now your employer is paying you.

Image and Substance

How you perform on the job is very important and much will be expected of you. In the workplace, it is essential that you recognize the importance of image.

The harder you work, the luckier you get.

Gary Player

In college, those who assign grades do not care much about your image. You were able to dress radically, doze through classes or not even attend them, party during the week, complain about the establishment, and so on. In some cases, those responsible for your grades never met you.

School is meant to be a time for self-exploration, and many unorthodox activities are tolerated as long as acceptable grades are maintained.

In the workplace, image becomes far more important. This may seem superficial to some graduates, particularly those with a bent for rebellion, but there are reasons for the importance of image. Many of the first impressions you make will be based upon image. These impressions affect how you are perceived by those within your organization, by clients or other people with whom you come into direct contact. These impressions project not only your image, but that of your entire organization. Image and your organization's attitude towards it, should never be treated lightly.

Being well organized is one indicator that you are adapting well to the world of work. Submit reports on time and keep your work area neat and uncluttered.

A major part of image is how you dress for the job. Clothing is important! Your attire is one of the first things people will notice about you and you must pay attention to it. You probably have not accumulated a vast collection of appropriate business attire and accessories by the time you graduate. You cannot however, expect to "get by", with the wardrobe that you pieced together for the recruiting campaign. You need to be able to dress appropriately the first day, the first week, the entire first month on the job. This means an up-front investment in clothing that will allow you to be suitably attired on a daily basis.

Remember what is deemed appropriate differs in each organization and often from one department or location to another within an organization. Your research prior to the recruiting process should now be expanded to finding out the dress code and getting specific advice as to what to wear. Respect the requirements at all times. Get in touch with people who've been recently hired in the organization and find out what type of clothing you should be wearing and if necessary, the best places in the area to shop.

Fashions fade – style is eternal.

Yves Saint Laurent

Orientation

Organizations will differ tremendously in the way they orient you. Some will start the orientation process the day they hire you. They will shower you with information about the organization and invite you to events and formal orientation programs prior to you beginning work. With other organizations, you may not hear from them from the time you are hired until the day you start work.

In both cases, and particularly the latter, you will have to work hard learning the corporate culture, how things are done and the work and management style.

The "Boss": ally or enemy?

Your boss is not like your school professors and should not be viewed as such. The professor had all the answers, encouraged argument and debate, laid out guidelines for assignments (usually well ahead of a due date) and was expected to be fair and objective. Your boss, on the other hand, often will expect you to get the answers. Some will discourage argument, will be vague as to how to complete a task and will regularly come up with last minute assignments, unclear priorities, vague directions and deadlines that you will regard as extremely unreasonable. The sooner you can accept this change from professor to boss, the easier your transition will be.

Your boss controls a great deal of what can happen to you during your first year. If you come into the organization with a terrific attitude, demonstrate poise and maturity, work well with others and apply both what you have learned at school and at the organization with an astute and enquiring mind, you will soon be chosen for the better assignments. If you fight the system, low level work may become your area of specialty. The more you complain about it, the more the boss will pile it on. The more enthusiastically you complete the grunt assignment, the more quickly you will be moved onto the better ones. Always be more than willing to do your fair share of any task or project and more. Thoughts like "it is not my job" or "I don't usually do things like that" should never enter your mind.

One of your biggest responsibilities in a new job is to make your boss, division, group and organization look good. This means completing work on time, ensuring that the quality is excellent, acting like a professional and maintaining a positive attitude. Keep your boss informed at all times of your progress and of any stumbling blocks you have encountered. Most like to be kept informed even though they may not constantly ask for progress reports.

Your boss and the organization, in return, are expected to train and develop you. Do not expect your boss to become your friend. And it is not recommended that you share your personal or financial problems with him or her. Being aware of your personal problems can affect the way he or she views you. Personal and professional lives should be kept separate. With any luck, your organization has a "neutral" sounding board (often someone in the Human Resources or Personnel Department) who can help you with these types of problems.

If you are initially working for a good organization but have a miserable supervisor, remember that your goal is to gain meaningful experience to move up in the organization. Chances are you will not have this boss forever. The idea is to perform as well as you can and learn as much as you can so that you can be promoted and move on. There are intolerable bosses, to be sure, but many graduates quit prematurely when faced with this dilemma. Your initial boss is rarely forever. If you can survive a year with a particularly tough supervisor, that can be a major feather in your cap. Before you lose your cool or take any rash steps that could jeopardize your career with the organization, take time to think things through. Remember, your work experience lives forever on your resume so you don't ever want to burn bridges.

Mistakes

Can you make a mistake? Yes, you can. Will you make a mistake? Probably. The secret to getting past it is to admit your mistake, then never make it again.

Subordinates

Many newly hired graduates have the idea that an army of subordinates will be on hand to perform all sorts of undesirable tasks. This is rarely the case. In fact, it is often the entry level graduate who is asked to photocopy reports, deliver memos, proof-read documents, tally columns of numbers, and even run errands. The better your attitude towards handling these seemingly menial chores, the sooner you advance from them. They are all part of "learning the ropes" and "paying your dues".

Too frequently, the new graduate arrives on the scene and treats the secretaries, sales clerks, production workers, technical aides or filing clerks as personal subordinates. If you fall into this pattern, you will probably jeopardize your potential to succeed. These employees are very well attuned to the arrogance of many new graduates. If they sense this arrogance in you they can respond in ways to make your life miserable. Never act in a conde-

Send a thank you letter after an interview... it gives you the opportunity to add information that you might not have remembered during the interview. It reminds an employer who you are and that you are still interested in the position.

Barry Koentges
Director, Student Employment
Centre, University of Calgary

When written in Chinese, the word crisis is composed of two characters. One represents danger and the other represents opportunity.

John F. Kennedy

184

scending or superior manner to those with less education or lower positions. It is unacceptable.

Treat all people fairly and well, extremely well, in fact. Develop a reputation for being a person with whom people enjoy working. Before you try to order a secretary to bring you your coffee, or drop a stack of papers on someone's desk and insist that it be copied in five minutes, think about how you would want to be treated if the situation were reversed.

When you're first hired, remember that subordinates are not at your beck and call. Many of them will have been in their jobs for years, are highly valued employees, and do not exist to cover the deficiencies in your background. They will not correct your spelling errors, or those other first-time errors you make, unless they like and respect you. You will soon learn that they can help you every step of the way.

Professionalism

A few other concerns should be mentioned in a category we will simply call "professionalism". They may seem obvious but they are violated by many new hires, hurting their careers. Do not fall into these traps.

Telephone use

Use of office time for personal telephone calls is taboo in most environments unless it's an emergency. Such calls should be kept to a minimum and should never be for social purposes during working hours. If it is really essential that you make personal calls, do so at lunch time and discreetly.

Clock watching

Do not just be on time for work. Be early! Do not leave at the closing bell. Stay after the formal quitting hour to read files, prepare memos or to clear your desk of paperwork. Managers quickly identify clock watchers. Do not get into the habit of making plans to meet with friends immediately following work. All too often, you will end up disappointing either your friends or your superiors because a last minute project came up.

One of the best ways to persuade others is with your ears – by listening to them.

Dean Rusk

Gossip

Most gossip is petty and inaccurate. It often arises from resentment or jealousy. Do not be part of it. No one trusts a gossip.

Politicking

No one appreciates the new hire who is sycophantic to the boss and to other managers. You can do your job well and let others know what you have done, but do not become a bootlicker. You'll quickly become the subject of ridicule.

Honesty

You will make mistakes now and then. Your supervisors expect this, but they will not want to be surprised as a result of a mistake. They'll appreciate your honesty and self confidence when you admit you're wrong.

Confidentiality

You may be in a situation where you deal with sensitive information about people, programs or products. Maintain an appropriate level of confidentiality. While you are certain to be proud of the information to which you have access, even your friends will respect your need for confidentiality and your inability to "give them details" or provide them with "scoops".

Drinking, drugs, and raucous behaviour

Never show up for work under the influence of either alcohol or drugs. Do what you like in your free time, but not on the job. Is your "off hours" behaviour your employer's concern? It is if it affects job performance or credibility. If it reflects on your maturity and advancement potential, they will make it their business.

Listening

One of the great professional skills you can develop is to give undivided attention to what others are saying. It is called active listening, and most people are not very good at it. You will find most people are more interested in what they have to say than what you have to offer. If you are a good listener, others will invariably think you are very bright. A good conversationalist gets others talking.

No man ever listened himself out of a job.

Calvin Coolidge

The Evaluation Process

Many professors base their grading on exam scores, projects, term papers or a combination thereof. Most don't care if you show up for class, as long as you can convince them, by the end of the semester, that you have learned the material. This might be fine on campus and you might have enjoyed the leniency and lack of structure, but recognize the fact that it is not accepted in the real world.

The end of a school term brings with it the typical push to finish term papers and reports, study for final exams, and then wait for grades. Grades become the measure of how you have done over a clearly defined period of time, based upon predetermined criteria. A couple of weeks later you begin new courses with new syllabuses and new professors. The slate is clean and you have a fresh start toward a new set of grades.

Your evaluations in your first job may be one of two extremes or anywhere in between. At one extreme they may be irregular, informal and vague or at the other extreme, they may be formal, regular and very sophisticated in structure and content. If you think grading in college can be unfair, wait until you find that a single two minute encounter with a client can colour your evaluation for an entire year.

Your boss will always be your evaluator, and whether or not your organization has a formal and systematic performance appraisal system, he or she will have the final say. Much of the evaluation will be based upon attitude, interpersonal skills, cooperation and reliability.

Regardless of the format of the performance appraisal system, almost any evaluation process will include some criticism of performance or behaviour. View this as a guide to direct your efforts. You might find that your boss's priorities do not match your own, but that is not cause for argument. Pay heed to your priorities, but make sure you concentrate on those suggested by your boss.

Some supervisors are very good at giving positive feedback on a regular and informal basis. It may be in the way they thank you for completing an assignment, or a reinforcing comment about how you met a client, or it may be an encouraging remark about how you dealt with a frustrating situation.

This kind of feedback is important. But be prepared for some supervisors who may never say anything good at all.

Equally important are the clues your boss might give you about how you can improve your performance. Offhand comments about the length of a memo, your attire, or your time spent on a personal telephone call should be taken seriously and the issue corrected immediately.

Unlike in a school environment where semesters end and you move on to a new set of courses and lecturers, results in the workplace are cumulative, and memories are long. It is not only your boss' opinion that is important, but those of others that can have an effect on your career, so your objective is to be regarded as highly as possible by as many people as possible.

Remember that someone with whom you only have a brief encounter today may be your boss, co-worker, or subordinate tomorrow. Your performance slate is not easily wiped clean.

Many new graduates are frustrated by the lack of grading and assessment they receive on the job. This is a major adjustment in entering the workplace. Grading on the job is rare, but your performance is being continually assessed so you need to be sensitive to this at all times. Good performance with even occasional lapses is viewed as a lack of dependability.

First Year Financial Management

Because entry level salaries, geographic area costs of living, personal financial situations and living arrangements vary so greatly, it is difficult to provide advice that applies to everyone. Pick and choose from the information below as it might apply to you. It will all be particularly relevant if you are going to be living away from your family.

Initial salaries for most college and university graduates are generally well above subsistence levels, but certainly not enough to be described as lavish. With reasonable financial management, most graduates can make it through their first year on the job without adding too much to their existing debt level.

Problems arise when graduates overestimate the spending power of their initial salary, while they seriously underestimate the start-up costs of beginning a new job. Many also forget the sizable portion of the salary that they will never see because of things like taxes, deducted at source. These combined misconceptions may lead you to commit to expenses you cannot handle. Examples: high rents, car payments, stereo equipment, furniture or clothing. Take a realistic view of how far your salary can go before making any major commitments.

It is not greedy or excessively materialistic to want nice new things, particularly after having a small income most of your life to date, and having to deprive yourself of many of life's luxuries. It is unrealistic to get everything you want immediately. Unfortunately, many graduates fall into this trap; a few months of excesses may lead to years of financial stress.

The best way to determine what you can afford is to develop a personal monthly budget and although it takes tremendous discipline, to live by it.

Start-up costs

It can be surprisingly expensive to get established in a new home. You should begin making these arrangements early so that you'll understand what costs are involved and what you can afford. You should be moved in and settled by the time you begin work.

Many graduates rent apartments. Apartments may require a month's rent as deposit and a month's rent in advance. In order to sign the lease on a $450 apartment, you may need as much $900 up front. Some apartments even require that the last month's rent be paid in advance, too. Others require a key deposit. Read your lease carefully before signing and make sure you understand what you will get for your money. If you have any doubts, ask friends or family for help.

Transportation

Before you do anything, ask the organization some important questions about transportation. Do you need a car for work? Do they supply one? Do they reimburse you for mileage driven for business purposes? Do they pay for parking? At the office? On the road? If you ask a room full of graduating seniors what item they want to purchase first upon accepting a job offer, the most frequent answer is invariably a new car. Some have no car, some have ancient clunkers, and others have had their eye on a particular model for a long time. My advice may not be what you want to hear, but could be crucial in keeping your head financially above water. Don't buy a new car until you have found out the transportation requirements of the job and you have lined up all your other budget items and know what you can afford.

By the way, as you calculate your monthly transportation budget, don't forget to include your auto insurance.

If you are fortunate, you will work in a place where parking is free. However, many new hires begin their careers in downtown locations where parking can be extremely expensive. Check with your employer to get an idea of what parking will cost you.

Income

In the first place, your take-home pay may not be quite what you expect. You will have a variety of deductions taken off before you get your share.

Find out what you can expect to take home each month. Gross pay is important, but it's the take-home that you have to live on.

Savings

Plan to save something. Even if it is only ten dollars each month, plan your budget so that there will be something to put aside. As your salary increases, you will increase your monthly savings, but it's great to get into the habit now. Keep this money separate from vacation savings, emergency funds, or other accounts that you tap into from time to time.

Planning your budget

Finally, with all the above points in mind, you are ready to plan your budget.

Begin your budget planning with necessities such as food, rent, clothing and transportation. Begin conservatively but still realistically. Then add in all the other items that contribute to your monthly expenses.

Some items such as furniture or clothing are easiest to calculate first on an annual basis, then break them down into monthly components. This is because some costs may be higher in some months than others so you need to plan based upon an average.

Now compare your estimated monthly expenses with your monthly take-home pay. If the expenses are higher, begin to adjust some items downward, but only with the idea that you will live by your plan. You may go through a number of drafts before you get a workable budget, but it's well worth the time and effort.

For at least the first few months on the job, try to keep a tally of expenses so that you can go back and adjust your budget where necessary. If you are spending more than you make, find areas where you can cut back, and do it promptly. If you are surprised at how much is left over each month, increase your savings. You can even start to think about one those luxury items that you passed by. The point is, manage your money!

A Real Life Case Study

14

As I headed towards the finish line in writing this book, a friend asked me to assist him in hiring an entry level human resources consultant. In exchange for using the replies to the advertisement for an in-depth analysis to be used in this book, I agreed to help him with the project.

The position

The position was described in the advertisement as a Human Resources Consulting position requiring no previous work experience.

The advertisement

The position was advertised in the "Professional Help Wanted" section of *The Montreal Gazette.* The advertisement called for applicants to send their resumes and a cover letter that "should include a 50-word paragraph stating why you are perfectly suited for the HR field".

Analysis of Replies

A total of 129 replies were received. I used the "resume and cover letter last minute checklists" to assess the replies and give you a look inside the actual recruiting for an entry level position.

Assessment of the cover letters

Was the letter typed?
>   **Yes** 86.8%   **No** 13.2%

Six of the seven handwritten replies were written on scraps of paper. One was written on the first page of the resume and two were illegible.

Was a good quality paper used?
>   **Yes** 52.7%   **No** 47.3%

In 25% of the cases the cover letters were on extremely high quality paper. Because of the overall poor quality these really stood out.

Were there spelling mistakes?
Yes 7.8%   **No** 92.2%

This is unforgivable, considering the fact that most people used computer software that has a "spell check" program.

Were there major grammatical errors?
Yes 22.5%   **No** 77.5%

I did not include minor errors in these results.

Was the cover letter visually appealing?
Yes 61.2%   **No** 38.8%

The 50 that I rated as unappealing were poorly photocopied, badly designed, had typing errors, used poor quality paper, were hand written or had errors corrected by hand.

Was the position to which they were applying clearly indicated?
Yes 91.2%   **No** 8.8%

Far too many candidates wrote the job title in by hand on a generic cover letter.

Did they include the "required" 50-word paragraph?
Yes 38%   **No** 62%

The fact that 80 people did not follow a simple instruction clearly stated in the advertisement should give you encouragement that the competition for entry level jobs can be beaten, if you follow the advice laid out in this book. Only 25 of the 49 people, who did write the paragraph, kept it between 45 and 55 words.

Did they sign the letter?
Yes 94.6%   **No** 5.4%

There is no explanation for this.

Did they tailor the letter to the position described in the advertisement?
Yes 77.5%   **No** 22.5%

All those that did not simply sent in a generic cover letter.

Was the envelope used professional and clean?
Yes 90%   **No** 10%

Assessment of the resumes

Of the 129 replies received, 127 people sent their resumes. One person who did not, indicated in his cover letter that he did not think it was necessary. The other person just chose not to include her resume.

Was a good quality paper used?
Yes 51.2%   **No** 48.8%

In almost all cases the paper was the same as that used in the cover letter.

Were there spelling mistakes?
Yes 8.5%   **No** 91.5%

The same comments concerning cover letters apply.

Was the resume visually appealing?
Yes 60.6%   **No** 39.4%

The biggest faults were in type styles chosen, the design of the resumes and the poor quality paper.

Did they include their name on each page of the resume?
Yes 45.7%   **No** 54.3%

Not a major issue but worthy of mention.

Did they include their skills and achievements?
Yes 38.6%   **No** 61.4%

It is amazing that over sixty percent of the applicants did not include anything on their unique skills or achievements in previous jobs, at school or in the community.

The Good, the Bad and the Ugly (revisited)

One candidate's first paragraph was 82 words long. It concluded with the following phrase: "this excellence I have acquired is my natural ability to understand people and their strength, weaknesses and potentials"

One candidate included a 8 1/2" x 14" resume. Throughout the process the bottom of the resume got crushed and mutilated.

One candidate pleaded "All I need is given the opportunity to prove my point". A phrase such as "I would appreciate the opportunity to be able to explain…" is far more appropriate.

One candidate stated, bold and underlined, that his long term career goal was "Manager – Production, Quality Control". Another stated that his "Occupational Objective" was "To make a contribution in the purchasing function within a progressive organization". This is hardly appropriate when applying for a human resources position.

It took one candidate eight years to complete CEGEP (the two year Quebec pre-university program) and a three year undergraduate degree, with no explanation as to why.

One resume included four different fonts on the first page. This was difficult to read and certainly not visually appealing.

One person concluded his cover letter with the following sentence "I you have any further questions as to how I can be of service to The *Gazette* please don't hesitate…". Besides the typing error, "I" instead of "if", did he really think the position was to work for the newspaper running the advertisement? What made it worse was the fact that the word "Gazette" was italicized, which meant that anyone reviewing the resume could not miss it.

The advertisement specifically asked candidates to include a "50-word paragraph" in their cover letters. One candidate's was 123 words, while another's was 139 words and one person's paragraph had just 10 words. The longest one had 168 words. This same candidate ended her cover letter as follows: "In conclusion if I had to pick six words which will best describe me I would have to list: hard working, good at taking the initiative, ambitious, loyal, outgoing and imaginative". Six words means six, not twelve.

One applicant did not include any dates with his work history, which included six positions. It made the resume extremely difficult to evaluate.

One candidate broke a "cardinal rule" and included a picture of himself.

Under the "achievements" heading, one candidate included "reading, cooking, repairing things and relaxing".

One person had obviously moved since her resume was prepared. Rather than retype it, she crossed it out with a pen and handwrote a new address. I envisaged her doing the same thing to a report for a client with a last minute change.

A candidate included this statement in his cover letter "I have recently completed my degree and I'm ready to put my skills to use for some lucky organization". He failed, however, to explain why the organization would be lucky.

One candidate wrote the following as his opening sentence in the 50-word paragraph: "Frankly, I am perfectly suited for the Human Resources field because I am good enough, I am smart enough and doggone it, I am worth it". A vague attempt at humour.

Another wrote "recently, in the job market, I have been very disappointed in the responses I have been getting from potential employers". Your cover letter is not the place to vent your job search frustrations.

Yet another candidate wrote: "I am seeking an entry-level position leading to a career with your firm, being aware of your excellent reputation and aggressive commitment to the industry". Interesting, but hardly sincere. The name of the company doing the hiring was never mentioned in the advertisement.

Many people in an effort to impress potential employers, use words and phrases with which they are not fully familiar. As a result they are unnatural and often don't make sense.

"Able to communicate ideas for self and others…"

"Facilitating understanding interpersonal skills"

"Individuals have great potential; they need somebody to discover them"

"Thank you very much for your utmost assistance for this matter and I am looking forward to hear…"

Keep positive! Do not get discouraged – a negative attitude will not lead to a job offer.

Ernie Hovell
Director, Career Planning &
Employment Centre,
Acadia University

"I trust that my interest in this field, will ensue the benefit of an interview"

"I was pleasantly surprised to see your innovative approach that you employed in order to fill the HR position. Refreshing indeed, for that your advertisement gives a fair chance to a person like me which while has all the educational qualifications and the immense desire to fill a HR position, but, unfortunately lacks previews service in the field"

"Turning a negative situation into a positive one is what I specialize in. This experience has served as a springboard and reservoir which has enabled me to draw upon and generalize to other problematic situations".

Words that were misspelled

Juli	July
Resourcefulnes	Resourcefulness
My self	Myself
Litterature	Literature
Recrute	Recruit
Concernes	Concerns
Interpersonnel skills	Interpersonal skills
Saterday	Saturday
Candidacacy	Candidacy
Strenghts	Strengths
Mayor	Major
Negociate	Negotiate
Benificial	Beneficial
Witch	Which

Which Resumes Were Selected?

The overall quality of the applications was generally regarded as poor but fairly consistent with responses to similar advertisements for entry level positions I've recently seen. Only nine resumes were selected for interviews. To conclude the study, I thought it would be useful to review how these 9 resumes scored on the "checklist evaluation criteria".

Assessment of the cover letters

Was the letter typed?
    Yes 100%

Was a good quality paper used?
    Yes 88.8%   **No** 11.2%

Were there spelling mistakes?
    No 100%

Were there major grammatical errors?
    No 100%

Was the cover letter visually appealing?
    Yes 88.8%   **No** 11.2%

Was the position to which they were applying clearly stated?
    Yes 88.8%   **No** 11.2%

Did they include the "required" 50-word paragraph?
    Yes 100%

Did they sign the letter?
    Yes 100%

Did they tailor the letter to the position described in the advertisement?
    Yes 100%

Was the envelope used professional and clean?
    Yes 100%

Assessment of the resumes

Was a good quality paper used?

Yes 88.8%   **No** 11.2%

Were there spelling mistakes?

No 100%

Was the resume visually appealing?

Yes 100%

Did they include their name one each page of the resume?

Yes 54.8%   **No** 45.2%

Did they include their skills and achievements?

Yes 100%

What lesson can be learned from this exercise? Does it mean you are guaranteed an interview if you follow all the suggestions on the last minute checklist? No, but as the study shows, it certainly increases your chances substantially if you take care and ensure you don't make silly mistakes.

The Conclusion

I hope you have enjoyed this book. Keep it close by and use it as your guide as you go on your job search adventure. Always keep in mind what gets the attention of recruiters and what will make them want to hire you. Remember that the quality of your first job will go a long way in determining your second and third. Be relentless in your pursuit and learn from each experience. Take your time making the decision and don't ever compromise your beliefs or principles.

And above all else… "To thine own self be true"

Good Luck!
Stephen Kaplan

Appendix I: Action Verbs

Consider using these action verbs as you write your cover letters, resumes and CACEE forms.

accelerated	catalogued	counselled
accomplished	chaired	created
achieved	charted	cultivated
acted	checked	decided
adapted	clarified	defined
addressed	classified	delegated
adjusted	coached	delivered
administered	collaborated	demonstrated
advertised	collected	designed
advised	communicated	detailed
allocated	compared	detected
analysed	compiled	determined
applied	completed	developed
appointed	composed	devised
appraised	computed	diagnosed
approved	conceived	directed
arranged	conceptualized	discovered
ascertained	condensed	dispensed
assembled	conducted	displayed
assessed	confirmed	disproved
assigned	conserved	dissected
attained	consolidated	distributed
audited	constructed	diverted
authored	consulted	documented
authorized	controlled	dramatized
balanced	cooperated	drew
budgeted	coordinated	drove
built	copied	dug
calculated	correlated	edited
canvassed	corresponded	effected

eliminated	illustrated	mentored
empathized	imagined	met
encouraged	implemented	modelled
enforced	improved	moderated
enlarged	improvised	modified
enlisted	increased	monitored
ensured	influenced	motivated
established	informed	navigated
estimated	initiated	negotiated
evaluated	innovated	observed
examined	inspected	obtained
executed	inspired	offered
expanded	installed	operated
expedited	instituted	ordered
experimented	instructed	organized
explained	integrated	originated
expressed	interacted	oversaw
extracted	interpreted	participated
facilitated	interviewed	perceived
filed	introduced	performed
financed	invented	persuaded
fixed	inventoried	photographed
followed	investigated	piloted
forecasted	judged	pinpointed
formulated	launched	planned
founded	learned	predicted
furnished	lectured	prepared
gained	led	prescribed
gathered	listened	presented
gave	logged	presided
generated	maintained	prioritised
guided	managed	printed
headed	manipulated	processed
helped	marketed	produced
hired	mastered	programmed
hypothesized	mediated	projected
identified	memorized	promoted

proofread
proposed
protected
proved
provided
publicized
published
purchased
queried
questioned
raised
realized
reasoned
received
recognized
recommended
reconciled
recorded
recruited
reduced
referred
regulated
rehabilitated
reinforced
related
rendered
reorganized
repaired
reported
represented
researched
resolved
responded
restored
retrieved
revamped
reviewed

revised
risked
scheduled
selected
sensed
separated
served
set
set up
shaped
shared
showed
simplified
sketched
sold
solicited
solved
spoke
standardized
stimulated
streamlined
structured
studied
summarized
supervised
supplied
supported
surveyed
symbolized
synergist
synthesized
systematized
taught
tended
tested
told
trained

transcribed
translated
travelled
troubleshoot
tutored
typed
understudied
undertook
unified
united
updated
upgraded
used
utilized
verbalized
verified
weighed
won
worked
wrote

Appendix II: Power Words and Phrases

The following is a list of "power" words and phrases you may want to consider using in your resume and cover letters. In each case, recruiters will expect you to prove these skills and attributes with examples.

ability to solve problems
accomplished
actively
adaptable
ambitious
analytical
appreciate the opportunity
articulate
astute
autonomous
business awareness
capacity
caring
competent
composed
conceptual skills
consistent
courageous
creativity
credible
curious
decisive
dependable
determined
eager
effectiveness
enterprising
enthusiastic
ethical

excellent communication and interpersonal skills
excellent time management skills
excellent leadership qualities
excellent memory
flexible
good judgement
hardworking
have excellent initiative
high energy level
honest
imaginative
independent
inquisitive
intelligent
inventive
keen eye for detail
loyal
malleable
moral
motivated
organized
original
persuasive
persistent
pertinent
poised
precise

proficient
proven track-record of success
qualified
resolute
resourceful
responsible
self-assured
self-reliant
self-starter
sensitive
sincere
spirited
strong background
substantially
take pride
team oriented
thrive on challenges
technically proficient
tenacious
trustworthy
versatile
vigorous
willing to accept change

Employment: Prohibited grounds of discrimination*

Canadian Human Rights Commission
Tel: (613) 995-1151
TTY: (613) 996-5211

Prohibited Grounds	Federal	British Columbia	Alberta	Saskatchewan	Manitoba	Ontario	Quebec	New Brunswick	Prince Edward Island	Nova Scotia	Newfoundland	Northwest Territories	Yukon
Race or colour	●	●	●	●	●	●	●	●	●	●	●	●	●
Religion or creed	●	●	●	●	●	●	●	●	●	●	●	●	●
Age	●	● (19-65)	● (18+)	● (18-64)	●	● (18-65)	●	●	●	●	● (19-65)	●	●
Sex (incl. pregnancy or childbirth)	●	●[1]	●	●	●[2]	●	●	●	●[1]	●	●[1]	●[1]	●
Marital status	●	●	●	●	●	●	●[3]	●	●	●	●	●	●
Physical/Mental handicap or disability	●	●	●	●	●	●	●	●	●	●	●	●	●
Sexual orientation	●[4]	●		●	●	●	●	●[1]	●	●[1]			●
National or ethnic origin (incl. linguistic background)	●			●[5]	●	●[6]	●	●	●	●	●	●[5]	●
Family status	●	●		●	●	●	●[3]			●		●	●
Dependence on alcohol or drug	●	●[1]	●[1]	●[1]	●[1]	●[1]		●[1,7]	●[1]	●[7]			
Ancestry or place of origin		●	●	●	●	●		●				●[5]	●
Political belief		●		●		●		●	●	●	●		●
Based on association					●	●		●	●				●
Pardoned conviction	●	●				●	●				●		
Record of criminal conviction		●					●						●
Source of income				●[8]	●					●			
Place of residence												●	
Assignment, attachment or seizure of pay											●		
Social condition/origin							●				●		
Language							●						

Harassment on any of the prohibited grounds is considered a form of discrimination.

* Any limitation, exclusion, denial or preference may be permitted if a bona fide occupational requirement can be demonstrated.
1) complaints accepted based on policy
2) includes gender-determined characteristics
3) Quebec uses the term "civil status"
4) pursuant to a 1992 Ontario Court of Appeal decision, the Canadian Human Rights Commission now accepts complaints on the ground of sexual orientation
5) defined as nationality
6) Ontario's Code includes only "citizenship"
7) previous dependence only
8) defined as "receipt of public assistance"

This document is also available on computer diskette and as a sound recording to ensure it is accessible to people who are blind or vision impaired.

Threatening, intimidating or discriminating against someone who has filed a complaint, or hampering a complaint investigation, is a violation of provincial human rights codes, and at the federal level is a criminal offence.

This chart is for quick reference only. For interpretation or further details, call the appropriate commission.

August 1993

Appendix IV: CACEE Membership List

The following organizations are current members of CACEE. For more information about employers listed below, speak to the Career Centre at your institution and consult the current *Career Options* magazine.

Employer Members

3M Canada Inc.

ADM-Agri Industries

AECL Research – Chalk River Laboratories

Agriculture Canada

Air Canada

Alan Davis & Associates

Alberta Treasury Branches

Allied Signal Aerospace Canada

Amoco Canada Petroleum Co. Ltd.

Amulet Consulting Ltd.

Andersen Consulting

Apotex Inc.

Arthur Andersen & Co.

Association des institutions d'enseignement secondaire (AIES)

AT&T Global Information Solutions

B.C. Telephone

Babcock & Wilcox

Bank of Montreal

Bank of Nova Scotia

BDO Dunwoody

Behaviour Description Technologies

Bell Canada

Bernard Hodes Advertising

CALA Communications

Canadian Hunter Exploration

Canadian Imperial Bank of Commerce

Canadian Olympic Association

Canadian Tire Corporation, Limited

Canadian Tire Acceptance

CDI Career Development Institute

Certified General Accountants

Chevron Canada Resources Limited

Cominco Ltd.

Consumer Impact Marketing Ltd.

Coopers & Lybrand

CP Rail System

CVE – Career & Vocational Evaluation Inc.

Day Advertising Inc.

Doane Raymond

Dow Chemical Canada Inc.

DuPont Canada Inc.

ECARS Rent-A-Car

EDS of Canada Ltd.

Employment & Immigration Library

Ernst & Young

Fluor Daniel Canada Ltd.

Foreign Services Exam/Career Counselling

FWJ Communications Ltd.

GCCA – Graduate Careers Council

GE Canada

Great West Life Assurance

Gulf Canada Resources Ltd.

Hoechst Canada Inc.

Honeywell Ltd.

Hong Kong Bank of Canada

Hughes Aircraft of Canada Limited

Human Resources Development Canada

IBM Canada Ltd.

Imperial Oil Limited
Ingram Micro Inc. (Canada)
IREG, Hydro-Quebec
KPMG Peat Marwick Thorne
London Life Insurances Co.
Mallette Maheu
Michelin Tires (Canada) Ltd.
Mintz & Partners
Mobil Oil Canada
MPR Teltech Ltd.
Northern Telecom Canada Ltd.
NOVA Corporation of Alberta
O.A.C.E.T.T. Ontario Association of
Certified Engineering Technicians
and Technologists
Ontario Hydro
Ortho-McNeil Inc.
PanCanadian Petroleum Ltd.
PMC – Sierra, Inc.
Price Waterhouse
Procter & Gamble
Public Service Commission of Canada
QIT – Fer et Titane Inc.
Research Dimensions Ltd.
Rexdale Microskills
Richter, Usher & Vineberg
Royal Bank of Canada
Schlumberger of Canada
Shell Canada Limited
Southwestern Company
SRAM – Service Régional d'admission du
Montréal Métropolotain
Sun Life of Canada
Syncrude Canada Ltd.
Techton Management Ltd.
The Mutual Group
The Society of Management Accountants
of Ontario

Toronto Fire Department
TransAlta Utilities Corporation
Trans Canada Credit Corp.
TransCanada Pipelines
tranSKILLS
Transport Canada
Union Gas Ltd.
Weyerhaeuser Canada Ltd.
Women Immigrants of London
Workers' Compensation Board
of Nova Scotia
Xerox Canada Inc.

Educational Institution Members

Acadia University
Alberta Vocational College
Algoma University College
Algonquin College
Alma Mater Society, UBC
Assiniboine Community College
Augustana University College
B.C. Institute of Technology
Bishop's University
Brandon University
Brock University
Cambrian College
Camosun College
Canadian College of Business & Language
Capilano College
Carleton University
CDI Career Development Institute
Cégep Ahunstsic
Cégep André-Laurendeau
Cégep Bois-de-Boulogne
Cégep de Chicoutimi
Cégep de Jonquière
Cégep de l'Abitibi-Témiscamingue

Cégep de la Pocatière
Cégep de Lévis-Lauzon
Cégep de Limoilou
Cégep de Rimouski
Cégep de Rivière-du-Loup
Cégep de Saint-Jérôme
Cégep de Sainte-Foy
Cégep de St. Félicien
Cégep de Trois-Rivières
Cégep du Québec à Chicoutimi
Cégep du Vieux-Montréal
Cégep Édouard-Montpetit
Cégep François-Xavier-Garneau
Cégep St-Jean-sur-Richelieu
Centennial College – Progress Campus
Collège d'Alma
Collège de la région de l'Amiante
Collège de Maisonneuve
Collège Moderne de Trois-Rivières
Collège Montmorency
Concordia University
Confederation College
Conestoga College
Dalhousie University
Dawson College
DeVry Institute of Technology
Durham College
East York Board of Education
École de Technologie Supérieure
École Polytechnique de Montréal
Fairview College
Fanshawe College
George Brown College
Grant MacEwan Community College
Groupe Collège LaSalle
Heritage College
Herzing Career College

Humber College
ICD, Institut Carrière et Développement Ltée.
Institut Herzing
International Academy of Merchandising & Design
Kelsey Institute – SIAST
Kwantlen College
Lakehead University
Lakeland College
Lambton College
Langara College
Laurentian University
Lethbridge Community College
Loyalist College
Malaspina University College
Marine Institute
McGill University
McMaster University
Memorial University of Newfoundland
Mohawk College
Mount Royal College
Mount Saint Vincent University
New Brunswick Community College
Niagara College
Nipissing University
Northern Alberta Institute of Technology
Northern College
Nova Scotia Agricultural College
Nova Scotia Community College
Okanagan University College
Ontario College of Art
Palliser Institute – SIAST
Peel Board of Education
Queen's University
Radio College of Canada
Red River Community College

Ryerson Polytechnic University

Saint Mary's University

Scarborough Centre for Alternative Studies

Seneca College

Sheridan College

Simon Fraser University

Sir Sandford Fleming College

South Winnipeg Technical Centre

Southern Alberta Institute of Technology

St. Clair College – Thames Campus

St. Francis Xavier University

St. Lawrence College

Sudbury Board of Education

Technical University of Nova Scotia

The University College of the Cariboo

Toronto School of Business

Trent University

Trinity Western University

Université de Montréal

Université d'Ottawa

Université de Sherbrooke

Université du Québec à Hull

Université du Québec à Montréal

Université du Québec à Trois-Rivières

Université du Québec en Abitibi-
Témiscamingue

Université Laval

University College of Cape Breton

University of Alberta

University of British Columbia

University of Calgary

University of Guelph

University of Lethbridge

University of Manitoba

University of New Brunswick

University of Northern British Columbia

University of Ottawa

University of Prince Edward Island

University of Regina

University of Saskatchewan

University of Toronto

University of Victoria

University of Waterloo

University of Western Ontario

University of Windsor

Vanier College

Wascana Institut – SIAST

Wilfrid Laurier University

York Board of Education

York University

Yukon College

The membership list is current as of
July 1, 1995.